1,88

12 $\frac{50}{Nmc}$

FAMOUS STARS
OF FILMDOM
(*Men*)

George Arliss

FAMOUS STARS OF FILMDOM
(*Men*)

by ELINOR HUGHES

*Illustrated from autographed
photographs*

Essay Index Reprint Series

Essay Index

originally published by

L. C. PAGE & COMPANY

BOOKS FOR LIBRARIES PRESS
FREEPORT, NEW YORK

First Published 1932
Reprinted 1970

STANDARD BOOK NUMBER:
8369-1518-6

LIBRARY OF CONGRESS CATALOG CARD NUMBER:
76-107716

PRINTED IN THE UNITED STATES OF AMERICA

To
Rebekah Hobbs

PREFACE

WITH the extraordinary advances in popularity made by motion pictures during the past few years, has come a demand for information concerning those men and women whose names mean money and whose faces, thrown upon the silver screen, are known, without exaggerating, all around the world. What they do, why they do it, what they wear, to whom they are married, what they did before they entered pictures, what their hobbies are, not to mention their likes and dislikes—all these questions are asked numberless times.

This book has been written in an endeavor to answer these questions: to answer them as fairly and honestly as diligent research and close attention to current events have made possible. Sensational "discoveries" have not lain within my scope or desire, for I have tried, in this volume and in the one which preceded it ("Famous Stars of Filmdom"—Women) to give a fair picture of the lives of these people and to set down the facts as I found them, without unfair prejudice or heightening of dubious rumors.

To choose the fifteen most prominent masculine stars of films today has not been an easy task, and those which I have not included may seem more important than those whom you will find in the following pages. If present plans are fulfilled, however, there will be other books to follow this, and in the end I trust that all will be given their rightful places. Popular taste changes almost over night in these swiftly-moving times, and new stars are brought forward to shine beside the old. Since, however, I am trying to be as comprehensive as possible, I have taken, so far as possible, those actors whose fame and popularity are of long endurance and whose names are as well known as household words. Whatever the future may hold for them, they deserve a place here, for they have built up standards of entertainment by which they are known all over the world.

Whatever may be the fate of this volume, I hope that the purpose which I had in writing it will be fulfilled: that the reader will be enabled to glean from it such information as will make possible greater enjoyment and greater understanding of the actors whom he has so often watched.

ELINOR HUGHES

January, 1932

CONTENTS

LIST OF ILLUSTRATIONS

GEORGE ARLISS

THE tremendous success of George Arliss in the talking picture world is something for which to be deeply grateful. Here is an actor who brings to the screen the suaveness, the assurance, the subtlety, and the ironic humor that for decades have made him famous in the theatre. Without exception, his films have been photographic versions of those plays in which he has been so successful on the stage. From filmdom's viewpoint, they bring nothing new in form or subject matter; to all appearances the camera has been placed among the footlights and allowed to photograph the limited sphere of action that the theatre allows. None the less, they are continuously interesting, even stimulating, and make more of an appeal to the intelligent spectator's interest than legions of tremendous spectacles. Unquestionably they would be of no importance whatever without Mr. Arliss. In some unfathomable manner, the secret of which is known only to himself, and perhaps not all of it, at that, he can so project his unique individuality onto the screen that one forgets the subject matter entirely and falls under the spell of his skillful, sometimes fantastic, but always compelling acting. He has made but four pictures, and yet he may at any time definitely leave the screen. Even so, the name of George Arliss has assumed a brilliance in the motion picture firmament on a par with his splendid reputation in the theatre.

When you come to consider the tremendous popularity that he has won with scarcely the lift of a finger, the fascination that he appears to have for audiences not demanding intellectual power and mental action, it is almost more surprising than it is gratifying. Mr. Arliss was not endowed by nature with any especial beauty of feature. In fact, all his life he has experienced difficulty in finding the sort of rôles to which he could adapt his personal idiosyncrasies and unusual appearance. He would be the first to deny any claim to personable features, yet the motion picture public—loath to accept homeliness save as an accompaniment to brute strength—has taken this small, delicately made man to its heart, flocks to his pictures, and, insatiable as Oliver Twist, keeps on crying for more. Mr. Arliss smiles serenely and makes his two pictures a year—without haste and without undue deliberation. Whatever he does, people will want to see, and he knows enough to husband his strength and at the same time to make himself the more desired by not appearing too often.

George Arliss was born in London, England, on April 10, 1868, the son of William Arliss-Andrews, a printer and publisher. From early youth, he cherished a keen desire to go on the stage and used to practice giving plays in the garret of his home. Not until he was eighteen years of age, however, did he dare to try his luck and venture forth in public. This historic debut was made at the Elephant and Castle Theatre, London, on September 18, 1886. His part was small, merely that of the gaoler in "Vidocq, the French Jonathan Wild," but it encouraged him to go on. For the next four years he remained at that theatre, under the management of J. A. Cave, playing every

6

imaginable sort of part in every conceivable kind of play, from operettas to the wildest of melodrama. On January 21, 1890, he made his first bow to the West End of London when he appeared at Terry's Theatre as Markham in "Across Her Path."

He was still having trouble in finding the right sort of parts, and decided to get away from London for a time in order to test himself in more difficult circumstances. Accordingly, he accepted an engagement, not a very brilliant one, to be sure, but chances were not too plentiful, to act in the provinces. For eight years he was away from London, acting in the big towns of England as well as the small, testing himself, and trying to see whether or not he could discover the niche where he really belonged. It was heartbreaking work, very uncertain, and often discouraging, but he had faith in himself and a determination to succeed in his profession, so he kept on, refusing to be daunted by hardships and setbacks. Finally he was called back to London by the Messrs. Gatti, managers of the Vaudeville Theatre, to play the rôle of Brumaire in "On and Off." This play opened in December, 1898, and proved the beginning of a two years' stay at that theatre.

Mr. Arliss had yet to achieve success to assure him of a permanent place in the theatre, but this long-wooed opportunity was close at hand, preceded by a most auspicious event. In the summer of 1899 he met a young actress, Florence Montgomery; they fell in love almost at first sight, and were married at Harrow Weald, England, on September 16, 1899. It is needless to remind those familiar with Mr. Arliss' career, how supremely happy and success-

8

ful was the marriage and how devoted Mr. and Mrs. Arliss have always been.

While playing with Mrs. Patrick Campbell at the Royalty Theatre, London, during the season of 1900-01, George Arliss made his first substantial hit, playing Keane in "Mr. and Mrs. Daventry." He soon followed this up by acting the Duke of St. Olpherts in "The Notorious Mrs. Ebbsmith," and Cayley Drummle in "The Second Mrs. Tanqueray." These rôles, coming in close succession, brought him the reputation of an expert actor of polite comedy drama, and attracted almost as much attention to him as was bestowed upon Mrs. Patrick Campbell, the star. Mrs. Campbell was so pleased with his work that she engaged him to come to America with her the following November. Accordingly, he made his first appearance in New York at the Republic Theatre in January, 1902, as Cayley Drummle in "The Second Mrs. Tanqueray." His acting made a great impression on New York theatre-goers and producers, so much so, indeed, that when his engagement with Mrs. Campbell came to an end, he was asked by David Belasco to assume an extremely important rôle in "The Darling of the Gods."

Very probably it was his performance in this play that won Mr. Arliss his reputation for playing sinister and smoothly evil parts. The drama was written by John Luther Long and Mr. Belasco himself for the use of Blanche Bates and told a tragic story of romance, treachery, and unwilling betrayal in old Japan. George Arliss took the part of Zakkuri, the crafty and evil minister of war, whose aim it is to destroy the outlaw lover of her heroine. He played with great force, fine imaginative skill and dramatic power that won him great acclaim. He fairly shared the acting honors when the drama opened at the Belasco Theatre, N. Y., on December 3, 1902. The play was a tremendous success, played in New York for months and then visited the leading cities of the country, winning acclaim wherever it was seen. A year or two later it was revived with Mr. Arliss and Miss Bates still in their original parts and achieved another considerable run at the Belasco Theatre.

After leaving Belasco, George Arliss went under the management of Harrison Grey Fiske and appeared with Mrs. Fiske in several interesting productions, notably "Becky Sharp," in which he played Lord Steyne, "Leah Kleschna," "Hedda Gabler," "Eyes of the Heart"—written by Mrs.

Fiske herself—and "The New York Idea."
For the season of 1907-1908 he was engaged
to play in repertoire with Mrs. Fiske, at
the Lyric Theatre, N. Y. Among the rôles
that he added to her repertoire was that
of Ulric Brendel in "Rosmersholm." This
engagement was followed by his appearance
at the Belasco Theatre, on August 18, 1908,
in the title rôle of Molnar's "The Devil,"
a play which he is soon to re-make as a
talking picture. This was one of his most
celebrated rôles and he played it for many
months. His next appearance was at the
Hackett Theatre, N. Y., on November 22,
1909, in the title rôle of "Septimus," a reasonably prosperous venture. Leaving New
York for a time, George Arliss then betook
himself to Chicago to play in "When We
Two Write History," on May 9, 1910.

This same year saw the real turning point

in his career. Among the plays submitted to him for his consideration was one entitled "Disraeli," written by the popular dramatist, Louis N. Parker. The subject appealed to Mr. Arliss and the possibilities of the character seemed great. Accordingly, he undertook the production of it, appearing for the first time in the title rôle on January 23, 1911, in Montreal. In view of its subsequent history, it seems hard to believe that the play was a semi-failure on its initial presentation, and Mr. Arliss, much discouraged, began to look around for another vehicle. Then the play began to pick up—it gained steadily in popularity as Mr. Arliss gradually brought it nearer and nearer to New York. When it opened in that city at Wallack's Theatre on September 18, 1911, after many successful months out of town, it created something of a furore.

In that play Mr. Arliss remained until the end of 1915. He has never had so sensationally profitable a venture, and the popularity of the play, the silent picture and the talking picture, speak volumes for his skill. It was the character of Disraeli as he unfolded it that made the success of the play. In his make-up uncannily like the pictures of Benjamin Disraeli, Lord Beaconsfield, in his later years, Mr. Arliss set before the public one of the crises of that picturesque statesman's career—the purchase of the Suez Canal. The playwright did not stick strictly to facts, but no one really minded. A pleasing touch was added to the production by the appearance of Mrs. Arliss in the rôle of Lady Beaconsfield.

Following "Disraeli," it was no small problem for George Arliss to find another play that the public would like as well. His choice was "Paganini," in which he appeared at the Blackstone Theatre, Chicago, in December, 1915. This drama about one of the strangest geniuses the world of music has ever known, served him for a year, and provided him with another opportunity for amazingly life-like reproduction of an historical figure. He took the play on tour and subsequently appeared in it at the Criterion Theatre, N. Y., in September, 1916. In New York the play did not last very long, so in the following February, 1917, he took the part of Professor Goodwillie in "The Professor's Love Story," a charming little comedy drama, utterly different from any of his preceding rôles. Turning once more to the past, he wrote, in collaboration with Mrs. Hamlin, the play called "Hamilton," describing certain phases in

15

the career of the great American statesman.
He had great fondness for the part and
played it for the better part of the season,
1917-1918, in New York and on tour, but
the public did not respond to it as heartily
as they had to some of his other vehicles,
perhaps because Mr. Arliss did not quite
convince them of his identity with the Alex-
ander Hamilton of history.

At the Century Theatre, in May, 1918, he
took part in a patriotic drama called "Out
There," in which he played the Doctor.
During 1919, he toured as Tom Kemp in
that biting satirical comedy, "The Mol-
lusc," and as Mr. Don in Barrie's poignant
little one-act play about an Englishman and
his dead soldier-son, "The Well-Remem-
bered Voice." In September, 1920, he
played at the Park Theatre, N. Y., in the
title rôle of "Poldekin," a curious and un-

satisfactory Russian play which failed to achieve a long run. Interestingly enough, Mr. Arliss was on the threshold of another of his most successful plays. This was "The Green Goddess," written by William Archer, the celebrated scholar and dramatic critic for his own amusement and to refute the popular theory that those who write about plays know not how to write them. With Mr. Arliss in the rôle of the sinister and bland Rajah of Rukh, "The Green Goddess" opened at the Booth Theatre, N. Y., in January, 1921, and made a tremendous success, both in that city and on tour. Subsequently Mr. Arliss took the play to London, a city which he had not visited for twenty-two years, and opened at the St. James Theatre, London, on September 6, 1923. Only too glad to see him again, London kept the play there for a full year, so that it was not until December, 1924, that New York had a chance to see him again.

He then appeared in "Old English," the dramatization of a short story of John Galsworthy. Mr. Arliss played the part of Sylvanus Heythorp, a grand old rascal, whose unscrupulous career was brought to an end by an act of charity. The author had in mind a very different type of man— a big, burly, red-faced personage—but Mr. Arliss created a Sylvanus within his own limitations, and made of him a remarkably vivid character. The play ran for some months in New York and later did extremely well on tour, during the seasons of 1925-1927.

In January, 1928, at the Broadhurst Theatre, under the management of Winthrop Ames, Mr. Arliss made his first venture into the classics, playing Shylock in Shakespeare's "The Merchant of Venice." In its physical aspects the production was very beautiful and historically proved to be an interesting experiment. Mr. Arliss' Shylock, however, bore too many traces of his individuality and too few of the character he portrayed. From an intellectual standpoint, it was admirable, but emotionally it left a good deal to be desired. Despite make-up and costume, despite a lucid reading of the lines, the spectator was conscious always of the actor as a punctilious English gentleman indulging in a masquerade. None the less, the production was reasonably popular in New York and something more than that on the road. One thing makes it of especial interest—it was the last stage rôle that Mr. Arliss took prior to devoting himself to motion pictures.

At the end of his tour in "The Merchant

of Venice," Mr. Arliss accepted an offer from Warner Brothers to star for them in a talking film of "Disraeli." It was a momentous decision, alike for actor and company. The film was made in Hollywood during the summer of 1929 and was released early in the autumn. Its success was both instantaneous and enormous. The public, tired of distressing experimental talking films, flocked to see a forceful player who was at once master of the English language and totally fearless of the microphone. George Arliss' quiet, sharply-edged acting, his clear, beautiful speech and the distinctive powers of his characterization, won him instant attention. The film achieved phenomenal runs all over the country and was voted the best picture of 1929 in the Film Daily's annual poll.

In the excitement of the success of this

film, many overlooked the fact that he had produced "Disraeli" as a silent film in 1921, and also had appeared before the camera in "The Green Goddess," "The Devil" and "The Conquering Power," after having played them on the stage.

"Disraeli" was followed by the talking version of "The Green Goddess," an interesting film, but not quite as exciting as it had been in the theatre. Nevertheless, Mr. Arliss's revengeful Rajah of Rukh, combining the educational advantages of the modern European with the barbaric savagery of the Dark Ages, was a striking and convincing portrayal. Next came "Old English," a dubious screen subject, one might think, owing to its lack of action, but a successful production. The picture turned out to be a character study, and not a story. The interest was centered entirely on Mr. Arliss, and he was successful even in eating a large meal before the camera and at the same time keeping audiences entertained. Everything he did was entirely in character —the character of a man accustomed always to having his own way, strong of mind, feeble of body, impatient of any weakness, and indomitable in the face of disgrace and death. This film was released in the autumn of 1930, after which Mr. Arliss went to England for a vacation, returning to take up work on "The Conquering Power" (released under the title of "The Millionaire"), the story of a wealthy man who satisfied a life-long ambition by leaving his gigantic concern to become a garage mechanic.

Gordon Craig once made the statement that a genius in the acting world will, by preference, choose plays that are not great in themselves and make them great by force of his gifts. To say that this is true of George Arliss may seem unjust, yet few will deny that the great majority of his plays have become popular due rather to his efforts than to their intrinsic merits.

Busy as his life has been, Mr. Arliss has found time to write several books, notably his extremely interesting autobiography, "Up the Years from Bloomsbury," published in 1927. Other works include "The Wild Rabbit," 1899; "There and Back," 1900; "The West End," (with Sir George Dance), 1902; "Widow's Weeds," 1910; "Hamilton," (with Mrs. Hamlin), 1917; "What Shall It Profit" (with Brander Matthews). In 1919 he was awarded the honorary degree of Master of Arts by Columbia University.

Mr. Arliss is not an easy person for whom

23

to find a play—his personality is too distinctive, his features too marked, and he is always at his best in parts that are distinctly out of the ordinary and that permit the development of certain individual traits and idiosyncrasies. Whatever George Arliss may be acting, whether on the stage or on the screen, he never shirks—you get the impression that he is giving the best that he has in him, not as a special favor, but as a matter of course. Audiences are quick to realize this and respond generously and appreciatively. Regardless of the field to which Mr. Arliss may choose to confine himself in the future, he will always win admiration, affection and respect. There is none to match him, and no one will question his right to be called great.

JOHN BARRYMORE

IT IS doubtful whether there is another actor of the stature and reputation of John Barrymore who treats his chosen profession with such apparent levity and with so little regard for its more serious aspects. The reason may be found in the fact that he was averse to acting in the beginning, preferring journalism and art, of a somewhat satirical variety. Yet he came of a family whose history was linked with the theatre. His father, Maurice Barrymore, was one of the handsomest and most popular matinee idols of his day. His mother, Georgie Drew, was not only an accomplished actress in her own right, but also a daughter of the celebrated Mrs. John Drew, whose "Mrs. Malaprop" is still affectionately remembered. His uncle, John Drew, was a celebrated actor. Although his older brother, Lionel, and his sister, Ethel, both took to the stage while still very young, John, the youngest of the family, seemed to have no histrionic leanings. Had he made a success of newspaper work, he would, perhaps, have avoided the theatre, but, according to his own humorous account, the editor for whom he first worked advised him to try some other occupation at once and to cease wasting copy paper and ink.

John Barrymore, or John Blythe, to give him the true and less sonorous family name, was born on the 15th of February, 1882. His education, while not always uninterrupted, was thorough. Considerable time was spent at Seton Hall, N. J., and later on at a school in London. Very early in

life he evinced an unusual gift for caricature and fantastically imaginative drawings, together, presumably, with the mor-
dantly clever wit that has served him so
well since then. As has already been suggested, no amount of persuasion could induce him to become an actor until he had
tried other work that appealed to him more.
He had hard sledding for a youngster still
in his teens and was often hard pressed to
know where the next day's meals were to
be had.

He tells a now fairly familiar but amusing story of those early days of experiment
and hardship. He happened to be in San
Francisco at the time of the terrible earthquake, but what annoyed him chiefly was
being dragged out of his comfortable bed
to assist in restoring the unfortunate city to
some semblance of order. After a strenu-

ous few days of digging in the ruins he wrote what he hoped was a very pathetic letter to his sister describing his hard and thankless life. She took it to their uncle, John Drew, who read it and returned it with the comment that: "It took an earthquake to get Jack out of bed, and the United States Army to make him work."

By 1903 he had at last grown tired of knocking about and decided that, since he wasn't much good at anything else, he would try acting. His first appearance on any stage was made at Cleveland's Theatre, Chicago, on October 31, 1903. The play was "Magda" and his rôle that of Max. Thus began, in an oddly serious fashion, what promised to be a career of happy-go-lucky comedy parts. In December of that same year he came to New York, appearing at the Savoy Theatre in

"Glad of It." At the Criterion Theatre, on April 4, 1904, he played Charley Hine in "The Dictator," and two months later tried his hand at Signor Valreali in "Yvette." The plays were not very important nor over successful, but they gave him a start at least.

The next year saw him in London, playing his original rôle in "The Dictator," but on this occasion his stay was brief. Returning to the United States, he toured as Jacky in "Sunday" and then, on December 25, 1905, was seen as Stephen Rollo in Barrie's "Alice Sit-by-the-Fire," and Pantaloon in "The Clown." This was followed by something called "Miss Civilization" and then by a tour to Australia. The head of the company was William Collier, an actor by no means unknown even in these forgetful days. Back in New York he succeeded the late Arnold Daly as Tony Allen in "The Boys of Company B," later taking this play on the road. In March, 1908, he played Lord Meadows in "Toddles" at the Savoy Theatre, and two months later was in Chicago appearing as Mac in "A Stubborn Cinderella," a play later brought to New York with Mr. Barrymore in his original part.

There did not seem to be any lack of work for him then any more than there is now, when the very rumor that he may return to the stage is enough to set Broadway and the hinterlands in a pleasant flutter of anticipation. Light comedy followed light comedy with varying success. Among the better known were "The Fortune Hunter," Gaiety Theatre, N. Y., September 4, 1909; "Uncle Sam," Liberty Theatre, N. Y., 1911; "A Slice of Life," February, 1912; "A

Thief For a Night," March, 1913; "The Affairs of Anatol," Little Theatre, N. Y., October, 1912; "Believe Me, Xantippe," 39th Street Theatre, N. Y., August, 1913; and "The Yellow Ticket," Eltinge Theatre, N. Y., January, 1914.

"Kick In," a comedy melodrama, at the Longacre Theatre, N. Y., in October, 1914, stands on the borderline between John Barrymore's comic and serious rôles, for the next important part that came his way was that of William Falder in "Justice," John Galsworthy's tragedy of the weakling in futile combat with the force of the law. It was his acting of this harrowing part that made his reputation as a serious actor, for the production—first offered at the Candler Theatre, N. Y., in April, 1916— was hailed as the outstanding artistic achievement of the theatrical season, and praise was fairly showered upon his head.

It is a curious thing how long it takes even the best of actors to establish a reputation that pays dividends at the box-office. For all the deserved acclaim bestowed upon him in "Justice," John Barrymore did not find his next play, for all its beauty and charm, an unmixed success. This was the famous "Peter Ibbetson," dramatized by Constance Collier from DuMaurier's novel and presented by her with John in the title rôle and herself playing Mary, Duchess of Towers. The play, presented in New York at the Republic Theatre in April, 1917, had a long run in that city, but when it ventured away from home the results were sometimes amusing and sometimes tragic. On one famous occasion "Peter Ibbetson" was played in Philadelphia to an audience of three persons. When

John sarcastically inquired of the doorman whence the valiant three had come,
he received the answer, in all seriousness,
that it was a pretty cold night and they
found the theatre pleasantly warm. Unlike his more celebrated forerunner, Edmund Kean, who incensed a scanty Boston
audience by refusing to play for them, John
Barrymore, with a wry smile, went on with
the performance.

Returning to New York, he appeared under the management of Arthur Hopkins at
the Plymouth Theatre in October, 1918, as
Fedor Vasilyevitch in Tolstoy's "Redemp-
tion," better known as "The Living Corpse."
This play, in spite of its somber theme, was
an eminently profitable venture, greatly
enchancing the reputations of star and manager alike. By this time, John Barrymore
was becoming known as a handsome actor

33

with an unexceptionable profile and who had an uncanny drawing ability. Men and women alike flocked to see him—the former because of his acting, the latter by reason of his romantic personal charm, and he gave every indication of rivaling his father as a matinee idol.

Still greater was the excitement when in April, 1919, Mr. Hopkins presented Sem Benelli's gruesome and spectacular melodrama, "The Jest," in which John and Lionel Barrymore co-starred. This ranks as one of the most brilliantly successful productions in many years and might have run indefinitely. The story was cruel, even ugly, the leading rôles unattractive but tempting, and the Barrymores took full advantage of them. John played Gianetto Malespini, a romantic Italian poet living in Florence at the time of the Medicis,

whose life was made almost unbearable by
the crude brutalities of a mercenary soldier,
Neri Chiaramentesi, played by Lionel.
Here the beautiful profile and the graceful
figure served John to fullest effect, and
the newspaper reports of the play com-
mented on his marvelous youthful beauty.
Mr. Barrymore, in his "Confessions of an
Actor," remarks sardonically that he felt
like "A stained glass window of an decadent
string bean." His apparent refusal to accept himself in the popular rôle of great
romantic lover struck many persons as
strange, and in view of his work in motion
pictures, seems even stranger to contem-
plate now.

"The Jest," after months in New York,
went out on the road, where it did phenom-
enally well. Then, all at once, John Barrymore exploded a bomb-shell. He told his

press-agent one day, just before going on for the performance, that "The Jest" would only continue for ten days more. After that the company was to set to work rehearsing Shakespeare's "Richard III." By that time, his word was practically law. The Benelli play came off the boards according to his ultimatum and the star plunged headlong into the work of preparing the rôle of the Duke of Gloucester. He had it ready in an unbelievably short time, and the production, designed by Robert Edmond Jones, was something of a sensation. The penalty for all this haste was a comparatively brief run. John Barrymore had exhausted his strength and could not endure so exacting a rôle for more than a few weeks.

The few weeks were enough, however, to establish him as one of the two leading

36

tragedians on the American stage, and without question the most conspicuous. Great and deserved as was the fame that he acquired from "Richard III," it was not enough to save him from the possibility of appearing in a failure. In April, 1921, at the Empire Theatre, New York, he appeared with his sister Ethel in something called "Clair de Lune." It was a dramatization by his wife, Michael Strange, of certain portions of Victor Hugo's novel, "L'Homme Qui Rit." Mr. Barrymore's rôle, impossible to believe as it may seem, was that of Gwynplane, the child who was stolen by gypsies and whose mouth was horribly mutilated. The unromantically inclined reviewers were quick to notice that Mr. Barrymore's makeup affected only one side of his face, the side, incidentally, which he turned away from the audience. Even

37

profiles may be better on one side than on
another, and Mr. Barrymore's is noticeably
handsomer when viewed from the left. Be
that as it may, the play was a failure, and
a very quick one, too. Not even his name
could carry a play of such slight dramatic
substance.

Undeterred by this, he turned next to
his most ambitious effort, the portrayal of
Hamlet. He had been contemplating the
venture for some time, but refused to attempt it without the assurance that he was
thoroughly prepared for it. After two
years of study, of watching the performances of other Hamlets of the time, notably
the wonderful rendition given by Walter
Hampden, and of training his voice, he felt
that the time had come. Early in November of 1922, Arthur Hopkins presented him
in "Hamlet" at the Sam H. Harris The-

John Barrymore

atre, New York. The wild applause that greeted the production overshadowed the praise lavished on "Richard III," and the play was the sensation of the year. None the less, after 101 performances, which surpassed the previous record set by Edwin Booth, Mr. Barrymore had had enough.

During the next season, however, he toured the United States with tremendous success and in February, 1925, played Hamlet in London to enthusiastic and appreciative audiences. Without much question, it is the best thing he ever did on the stage, and the part by which he best deserves to be remembered. That there were some dissenting voices in the chorus of praise is not altogether surprising, for there never has been and never can be a Hamlet to satisfy everyone. Those who did not particularly enjoy his portrayal of the rôle based their objections chiefly upon the hard and glittering brilliance of his acting, which left any affection or sympathy for the character altogether out of the question. He seemed at times excessively theatrical and too much given to striking poses. The production itself, an elaborate and handsome piece of work, was marred by the too evident efforts of the other players to concede him the center of the stage at all times. It was none the less a memorable piece of work and one that raised high hopes for John Barrymore's future in the American theatre.

With a disconcerting suddenness, however, he deserted the stage for the screen, and holds out little hope of ever returning to the scene of his former fame. Before leaving the theatre altogether, he had made one or two films, among them being "Dr.

Jekyll and Mr. Hyde," and "Sherlock Holmes." These two productions were notably artistic and opened up further possibilities for added fame and profit. Then, with the screening of "Beau Brummell," his finest film to date, John Barrymore definitely left the theatre and embarked on a new career. For the majority of his pictures he was under contract to United Artists, and for them he made, beside those already mentioned, "The Sea Beast" ("Moby Dick"), "When a Man Loves" ("Manon Lescaut"), "The Beloved Rogue," "Tempest" and "Eternal Love." More recently he has been under contract to Warner Brothers.

His films for this company include a brief and extraordinary appearance in "The Show of Shows," when he recited some passages from "Richard III" with full enjoyment of their melodramatic quality and also, to be quite truthful, with disconcerting exaggerations. The occasion was important, however, in that it was the first time that his speaking voice was heard by screen audiences. His first full-length talking film was a picturesque romance of 18th century Europe, written by George Preedy and entitled: "General Crack." The production was very handsome and enjoyed a considerable success, and Mr. Barrymore gave an interesting, somewhat florid portrayal in the leading rôle. He even sang a theme song, somewhat to the surprise of the spectator. "General Crack" was succeeded by "The Man From Blankley's," a whimsical and amusing little comedy in which the star, for the first time on the screen, appeared in modern dress. The film achieved only a *success d'estime,* for the public did not quite know what to make of it, but it gave John Barrymore the welcome opportunity to disport himself once more in satirical vein, a branch of acting in which he was notably successful on the stage.

With the comparative failure of "The Man From Blankley's" behind him, the actor turned his hand to something more spectacular and, hence, more destined to attract the public fancy. This was his old love, "Moby Dick," which he now remade with sound and audible speech. As was the case with "The Sea Beast" but little of Herman Melville's wonderful story was left. There was still a pretty heroine, a villainous brother and a happy ending, and Mr. Barrymore continued to undergo excruciating agonies of mind and body. Even in mutilated form, however, it was almost too grim for popular taste.

43

Having once embarked upon the classics, he could not change yet awhile, and the next celebrated story he decided to try was "Trilby," George DuMaurier's romantic novel of the Latin Quarter of Paris during the middle 19th century. This fantastic story, which has its roots, in fact, none the less, offered him the chance to play Svengali, the musician whose twisted soul could find expression only through the lips of the women he loved in vain. In screen form, the story became "Svengali," for the rôle of Trilby was given to an unknown seventeen-year-old girl named Marian Marsh. The picture was interesting in so far as John Barrymore's individual performance was concerned, but suffered from the unwarrantable distortions of the novel. Svengali was portrayed as fantastic, evil, sardonic, occasionally pitiable, but never did he become the grotesque, distorted personage imagined by DuMaurier. The characterization was consistent as it stood, nevertheless, and deserves to rank as a definite achievement.

Mr. Barrymore's most recently completed film is "The Mad Genius." Here once more he plays a thwarted artist, but one of a different sort. He portrays the son of a famous dancer in the Russian ballet, crippled hopelessly and unable to dance a step himself, who finds his only chance of fulfillment in the success of a brilliant pupil. Following this production, he remained inactive for a few months and then went to Metro-Goldwyn-Mayer to appear in "Arsene Lupin," with his brother, Lionel, an occasion which marked their first joint appearance since the days of "The Jest." He is fond of hunting—and, also, when not working, takes trips on his

45

yacht. It is likely, however, that if he continues in films, he will retain his privileges of choosing his stories and the important members of his casts. For several years now he has amused himself making films in which he plays variations upon the Jekyll and Hyde theme. One may regret a certain sameness about his characterizations, but at least they always avoid the pitfall of dullness.

Unless he should decide to return to the stage, it is not likely that he will leave California, for that state offers him much that is pleasant. It was there that he met his present wife, Dolores Costello, during the screening of "The Sea Beast." Previously, he was twice married: to Katherine Corri Harris and later to Mrs. Leonard Thomas, usually known by her pen name of Michael Strange. He has two daugh-

ters, Joan, by his second marriage and Dolores Ethel Mae by his third. Happily
married, with an income ample enough to
permit him to indulge in the occupations
he enjoys, and with all the work he wants
whenever he says the word, John Barrymore
need apologize to no one for living his life
in the way that most appeals to him.

RICHARD BARTHELMESS

THERE is one very definite impression
that one always receives from the acting of
Richard Barthelmess: he is utterly in earnest, honestly and genuinely trying to give
his best. One may not like all his pictures;
one may wonder, perhaps, why he chose
them, but one knows without the shadow
of a doubt that he is not going to turn out
a slipshod piece of work. He has his limitations, chief among them being a not too
active sense of humor, but the majority of
his performances make one feel that what is
being witnessed is life and not make-believe.
A player who is not positive of the correct-
ness of his presentation, cannot convince
others, but Richard Barthelmess is so sure

of his characterization that one is convinced
of its veracity, even though one may not
always agree with his interpretation.   In
the many years he has been on the screen,
he has yet to turn in a slipshod piece of
acting.   He may not always be brilliant,
but he is invariably sincere.

Richard Semler Barthelmess was born in
New York City on May 9, 1895. When
he was only two years of age, his father
died and his mother had to find work to
support herself and her young son.   She
went on the stage under the name of Caro-
line Harris, and, in view of later develop-
ments, it is also interesting to remember that
it was she who taught the Russian actress,
Alla Nazimova, to speak English when the
latter first came to this country. Young
Richard received his education in the public schools of New York, followed by a term

at the Hudson Military Academy and three years at Trinity College, Hartford, Connecticut. It was while still at college that he began to evince an interest in matters pertaining to the theatre. He became president of "The Jesters," the college dramatic club, and frequently served as leading man, stage director, and general handy man. Beside this, he sang in the glee club and incidentally cherished the desire to become an author. Evidently he did not waste his spare time at college, for in addition to acting and singing, he was senior cheer leader, vice-president of his class in 1917, and a member of Beta Beta chapter of Psi Upsilon fraternity, to which he still belongs.

The literary career upon which Richard was prepared to embark was discarded abruptly during the summer vacation preceding his senior year. He had begun to

develop an interest in films and had played
several minor rôles, but not until Nazimova,
because of her friendship for his mother,
and her interest in his work, gave him a
leading rôle in her production of "War
Brides," did the screen appear to offer a
possible future. Therefore, while the two-
reel Biograph production, "Gloria's Romance," may claim the distinction of being
his first picture, it is to "War Brides," that
his coming fame was due. This somber
war drama was considered quite sensational
at the time that it was made, and the players in it received a great deal of attention.
His success determined Richard to leave
his college career unfinished and enter motion pictures at once.

His first assignment of real importance
was as leading man for Marguerite Clark
in "Bab's Diary," "Seven Swans," and sev-

eral other pictures, but he did not accomplish anything particularly notable until he met David Wark Griffith, who engaged him to play in "The Idol Dancer," "The Love Flower," "Broken Blossoms," and "Way Down East." It was in "Broken Blossoms" that he gave what may easily remain his most celebrated performance, matched only by his work in "Tol'able David." "Broken Blossoms" is the story by Thomas Burke entitled "The Chink and the Child," a drab, infinitely pitiful drama, which Mr. Griffith handled in marvelous fashion. Richard Barthelmess played the young Chinaman who rescues the frail "L'il Lucia" from the savage brutality of her drunken father, brings her home with him, and for three days of paradise treats her as a little goddess. The tragic ending of the idyll is too well known to need repeti-

tion here, but it is safe to say that the actor
has never surpassed his portrayal of the
gentle, meek Chinese boy, who could be
as tender as a woman toward the child
whom he adored, and as cruel as a demon
to the man who killed her. The picture
is still remembered, still talked about,
though it was released in 1919. In "Way
Down East," which followed, Richard gave
another excellent performance, but was less
prominently cast, for the film was designed
to star Lillian Gish. In those scenes in
which he appeared, one saw a handsome,
sensitive, appealing young man, whose
crooked, wistful smile added much to the
charm of his expression.

By now, the name of Richard Barthelmess had come to mean so much in pictures
that a special company, Inspiration Pictures, was formed for the sole purpose of

starring him. The undertaking made one of the most auspicious starts known to film history, for the first production was none other than "Tol'able David." This picture, which won the Photoplay gold medal for 1921, was made under the direction of Henry King, later to become famous but at that time practically unknown. A better combination of director and star would be hard to find in a film, and between them they produced what is to this day considered a classic. The story, made more familiar by the recent talking film, is set in the Kentucky mountains, and the characters are simple mountain folk. The acting of Richard Barthelmess in the part of David Kinemon, the gentle, affectionate boy, forced into combat with the appalling Hatburns, emerging victorious, and no longer "just tol'able," will not soon be for-

Richard Barthelmess

gotten. Into his portrayal he put extraordinary truth, desperate feeling, and truly remarkable sympathy and understanding. One could not see the film and quite believe that it was make-believe, for it carried the stamp, not only of true drama, but of life itself. "Tol'able David" accomplished many things: it established Richard Barthelmess as a star of the first magnitude, it placed Henry King in the front rank of directors, and it introduced the unhandsome countenance and fine ability of Ernest Torrence to the screen world.

It of course seemed inevitable that so startling a beginning should be followed by a series of masterpieces, but that this did not prove to be the case should not cause any particular dismay. Good pictures followed hard on the heels of "Tol'able David," but they were not quite in the same class. Among them were "Fury," "Sonny," "The Bond Boy," "The Fighting Blade," "The Beautiful City," "Seventh Day," "Twenty One," "The Bright Shawl," "New Toys," "Just Suppose," "Ranson's Folly," "The Enchanted Cottage," "The White Black Sheep," "The Amateur Gentleman," "Classmates," "Shore Leave," and "Soul Fire." This list comprises a variety of subjects, some modeled on ideas suggested by "Tol'able David," others dealing with romantic periods of the past, and still others with the quixotic behavior of very noble young Englishmen who assume the responsibility for others' misdeeds and in the end vindicate themselves in triumphant fashion.

"The Fighting Blade" found Richard as a stern young Puritan soldier in Cromwell's army, and allowed him to indulge in his fondness for picturesque costumes and sword play. "The Amateur Gentleman," set in nineteenth century England, saw him playing the son of a prizefighter, who inherits a fortune and sets out to be a leading light in society, win a horse race, and marry a beautiful lady. It was adapted from the novel by Jeffery Farnol and proved a pleasantly romantic interlude in a series of sternly realistic dramas. "The Bright Shawl," although not altogether successful, was none the less an interesting screen adaptation of Joseph Hergesheimer's novel of the same name. "Just Suppose" was a poignant little story dealing with the visit to the United States of an heir-apparent to the British crown and his love for an American girl whom he is forced to renounce. It has proved successful on the stage as well as on the screen.

"The White Black Sheep" has a self-explanatory title, and Richard Barthelmess prefers not to think too much about it, holding it to be the worst thing he ever did. Of another color was "The Enchanted Cottage," a very poignant, fantastic little picture that was too delicate to get very far with the public. A crippled soldier, sensitive over being disfigured by injuries received during the war, retires to a small English village where he meets and loves a sympathetic, homely young teacher. They fall in love and suddenly see themselves as beautiful in one another's eyes. The world cannot see any difference in them, the soldier's relatives think him out of his mind, but to him and to the girl the miracle persists. From the nature of its subject, the picture was not destined for great popularity, but it was, nevertheless, a courageous and worthwhile venture. Another interesting experiment was "Shore Leave," one of the few excursions that Richard made into straight comedy. The subject, being the same as served "Hit the Deck" on the musical comedy stage and on the talking screen, needs no retelling, but in the leading rôles, Richard Barthelmess and Dorothy Mackaill contributed two delightful characterizations. "Classmates" was a story of West Point, and "Soul Fire" dealt sympathetically with the trials of a young composer trying to find his inspiration.

"Soul Fire" was the last of the pictures Richard Barthelmess made for Inspiration Pictures. In 1926 he was placed under direct contract to First National Pictures, an organization through which his films had previously been released. The first film he

59

made for his new management was "The Patent Leather Kid," a rather didactic but well acted and interesting story of a prize-fighter who is drafted into the army, displays a cowardly streak, but finally learns the meaning of patriotism and redeems himself. This was followed by "The Drop Kick," one of the familiar brand of football yarns, and then by "The Noose." The latter was a somewhat grim tale of a young desperado, sentenced to death for a murder he had not committed by the same judge who had officiated at his mother's marriage. Although a shade too gentlemanly for the criminal type, Richard, nevertheless, gave a strong and convincing performance. "The Little Shepherd of Kingdom Come," taken from the popular novel by John Fox, failed to achieve the success which might have been expected, owing to over leisurely development and a rather thin plot. After this came "The Wheel of Chance," "Out of the Ruins," "Scarlet Seas," and "Weary River."

This last-named film was the actor's first venture into talking pictures, and caused more than little excitement when the public discovered that he had used a voice-double for the song which gave the picture its name. The star's good speaking voice, even though unsuitable for singing, soon allayed suspicion, and his work in "Drag" aided in putting an end to any doubts of his capability for sound pictures. "Drag" was the interesting, pertinent story of a young man who finds that members of the family of the girl he has married are an almost insupportable drag on his time, his strength and his ambition. "Young Nowheres," his third talking picture, was a drab little tale

61

of two forlorn waifs, in love with one another but with no place to be alone, no prospects of being able to marry, and nothing to call their own but their devotion. It was a quiet, simple story, but beautifully acted and decidedly an artistic success. The playing of Richard Barthelmess and Marian Nixon was so exquisite that their presence on the screen, unsupported, for three quarters of the picture, was not tiring.

With "The Song of the Gods," the actor went back to the time of "Broken Blossoms" and once more took the part of a young Chinaman, this time, however, of a youth of wealth and social importance. The part was not an easy assignment and the entire cast was handicapped by the necessity of making the hero white instead of yellow, in order that he might marry the heroine. While Richard gave his custom-

ary, reliable, earnest performance, the main
significance of the film was the return to
the screen of Constance Bennett, who did
excellently with the rôle of the spoiled,
selfish, headstrong girl, who horsewhips the
man she loves, thinking him a Chinaman,
and then in remorse and humility, comes
back to beg his forgiveness.

In the summer of 1930 came "The Dawn
Patrol," considered by many to be one of
the best things that Richard Barthelmess
has ever done. It is a somber, tragic war
story, with no women, no sentimental com-
pensations, and no happy ending. Remi-
niscent perhaps, of "Journey's End," it sets
forth the brief lives of a group of young
British aviators, sent out against the enemy
in flimsy, badly equipped planes. In-
evitably, the tragic futility of it all turns
friends into enemies, makes the men reck-

less in the face of certain death, and finally leaves them resigned to accept whatever comes without protest. The work of Richard Barthelmess and Douglas Fairbanks, Jr., in the two leading parts, earned them the greatest possible recognition, and won stardom for the latter. It took courage to make a film of this sort, but its popularity justified the effort, and while it failed to be included among the best ten pictures of 1929-1930, it was, however, eleventh on the list.

Another interesting venture made by Mr. Barthelmess is "The Finger Points," which followed "The Lash,"—a leisurely romantic drama of old California. "The Finger Points" dealt, by implication, with the murder of Jake Lingle, the Chicago reporter, and, while timely in subject, is not altogether convincing in fulfillment. The

64

star plays the part of a reporter who extracts huge sums from leading criminal organizations under the threat of exposing their activities in his newspaper. His extortion finally goes so far that it leads to his death. "The Finger Points" was followed by "The Last Flight," the ironic story of a group of aviators who find themselves at loose ends when the Armistice brings their wild and reckless living to a close. It is the development of a novel by John Monk Saunders.

Richard Barthelmess is five feet, ten inches tall. His hair is black and his eyes are brown. Aside from his career, his hobby is travel. He has been to France, England, Switzerland, Hawaii, Mexico, Bermuda, Cuba, and Canada, but prefers New York to any other place in the world. He has an apartment there, in addition to maintaining a house in Beverly Hills, California. Among his favorite sports are swimming, riding, tennis, hunting, and yachting. He is fond of football, as a spectator, and likes bridge, the radio, the opera and all sorts of music. Never a publicity seeker, he dodges personal appearances, interviews, first nights and posing for portraits. He claims to be more interested in characterization than in the plots of his pictures, and cherishes the ambition to portray Napoleon on the screen.

During the making of "Way Down East" he met and, shortly afterward, married Mary Hay. Their marriage came to an end in 1927, and he is now married to the former Mrs. Jessica Haynes Sargeant of New York. He has one child by his first marriage, Mary Hay Barthelmess, now seven years old.

Popularity is something for which Richard Barthelmess has worked hard and honestly, and something which he thoroughly deserves. It is an accomplishment to remain before the public as long as he has been able to do and still have a steady and loyal following. He has done this by always playing fair.

WARNER BAXTER

PROBABLY more than any other actor on the screen Warner Baxter has reason to be grateful for the coming of the talking picture. He found films hard to get into and somewhat precarious going, until he was able to use his voice. "In Old Arizona," which many thought would finish his career, made his fortune instead, for it revealed hitherto unsuspected possibilities of characterization and romantic illusion, coupled with an infectious and delightful sense of humor which had been lacking in much of his work for the silent screen. He is at present in an enviable position, having more parts offered him than he can possibly accept, and being known and liked all over the country. Yet there was a period when he tried in vain for six months to get into motion pictures and finally had to give up in despair. His struggle for recognition is merely an indication that there is no formula for screen success: a fortunate few reach the top overnight, some fight all their lives and get nowhere, while others have to work hard but reap eventually a well-earned reward. From all indications, Mr. Baxter belongs in this last group.

Warner Baxter was born at Columbus, Ohio, on the twenty-ninth of March, 1893. There was nothing in his ancestry to predispose him to the stage, yet by the time he was ten years old, he had begun to show a predilection for the footlights. His father, a banker, had died when Warner was less than a year old, and his mother, while she disapproved of her son's chosen career, could do little to prevent him from following his own inclinations. During his years in high school he took part in many plays and before graduation was being regularly assigned to the leading rôles. When not acting, he was either rehearsing or writing plays and songs. His fine voice, which he took considerable pains to develop, stood him in good stead, and he found himself in great demand as an entertainer before his schooling had come to an end.

His mother wished him to complete a college course, but Warner was determined to seek a career in the theatre at once. However, circumstances forced him to compromise by becoming a salesman, and he entered the employ of a firm that manufactured farming implements. He did not enjoy this work over much, and when the chance came to try something else, he welcomed it with joy, especially since it afforded him an opportunity to act. The new opening came about very unexpectedly, somewhat after the manner in which such things happen in novels. Dorothy Shoemaker, playing a vaudeville act in Columbus, was faced with the problem of finding a new leading man between Saturday night and Monday afternoon, as her regular partner was taken ill without warning. A friend of Warner's, who was also acquainted with Miss Shoemaker, heard of her predicament and suggested that she might try Warner in the emergency. She interviewed him, decided that he would do, and spent the next thirty-six hours with him in frantic rehearsals. There were two songs to learn and quite a bit of dialogue to memorize, but Warner measured up to the task and opened successfully with Miss Shoemaker in Louisville, Kentucky, on the appointed Monday afternoon. He remained with the act for two months thereafter until his mother became so distressed that upon her insistence he gave up playing and returned home.

If he was not to be allowed to act, Warner of course had to do something else, so he turned next to the insurance business and became an agent for the Travelers' Insurance Company in their Philadelphia branch. This work also failed to appeal to him, so after saving his money for some months he gave up his insurance activities and invested all his savings in a half interest in a garage in Tulsa, Oklahoma. Apparently the fates were determined that he should not be a business man, however, for every cent of the money was lost and Warner was again out of employment and in reduced circumstances. This time, however, he did not compromise about the future. He was going to act; it was what he wanted to do and it was, furthermore, the only occupation in which he had achieved success. Accordingly, he joined the North Brothers Stock Company in Dallas, Texas, and with that organization he played a steady round of juvenile rôles for a period of two years. At the end of that time he was made leading man, receiving a salary of thirty dollars a week which was then quite satisfactory. Living must have been a bit less expensive in those days, for Warner was able before long to save up sufficient money to go to California and try his hand at motion pictures. He spent six months in a vain endeavor to get the casting directors to even notice him. It was no use. With his clothes becoming threadbare and no prospect of screen work in sight, he for-

73

sook Hollywood and joined the Burbank Stock Company.

He remained with this company for seven years before he was observed by Oliver Morosco, the theatrical producer, who was impressed with his acting and engaged him for a feature rôle in "Lombardi, Ltd." After a preliminary run in Los Angeles starting July 1, 1917, the play opened in New York on September 22, and on that same day Warner married Miss Winifred Bryson who was also a member of the cast. Leo Carrillo had the leading part and the play ran for several months. In December, 1918, the play was presented at the Plymouth Theatre in Boston, and was then sent west once more. Warner's part was that of a young Italian, a newly rich, friend of the impractical hero. He played it with excellent spirit. Mr. Morosco liked his work, and when "Lombardi, Ltd." came to a close, he sent Warner to Los Angeles to take leading parts in the Morosco Stock Company, then playing at the Majestic Theatre. This looked like the beginning of some really promising things, but fate had different ideas in mind.

Warner had scarcely stepped off the train that took him to California when a motion picture writer, Elmer Harris, caught sight of him and urged him to enter filmdom. If he was amused or surprised, Warner made no especial ado over the matter and promptly accepted the offer. His first rôle was one of the leading parts in "Her Own Money," a Paramount production starring Ethel Clayton. Hardly had he started work on the picture when the Morosco company, to which he was still under contract, called him for rehearsals of "A Tailor Made

75

Man." There was nothing for him to do but take part in both play and picture, so for weeks he was acting day and night. This was a rather strenuous program, however, and before long he decided to give up the stage and devote himself entirely to the screen.

Then there began a period of several years in which he played in every sort of story from drama to comedy, and from tragedy to farce. He supported Bebe Daniels, Dolores Del Rio, Gilda Gray, Martha Sleeper, Patsy Ruth Miller, Margaret Livingston, Lon Chaney, and many other prominent players. While his work was satisfactory it did not attract any particular attention. In 1926 he played in "Mannequin," "The Runaway," "Aloma of the South Seas," "The Great Gatsby," "Miss Brewster's Millions," and "Mismates."

76

"Aloma of the South Seas" marked something of a departure, for it was one of those tropical dramas in which Warner portrayed the native lover of a beautiful dancing girl temporarily enamored of a white man. He made a handsome South Sea Islander, but his rôle was not particularly important. "Miss Brewster's Millions" found him playing with Bebe Daniels in an adaptation of the popular comedy, "Brewster's Millions," a story of the difficulties experienced by a young man, (or woman, as the picture had it), in disposing of one fortune in order to inherit another. "The Great Gatsby," taken from a novel by F. Scott Fitzgerald, discussed the problems of a man raised by his war service to a place above his former social status.

In 1927 he appeared in "The Telephone Girl," "Singed," "Drums of the Desert," and "The Coward." The year 1928 brought "The Tragedy of Youth," "A Woman's Way," "Ramona," "Craig's Wife," "West of Zanzibar," and "Danger Street." "A Woman's Way" was a highly melodramatic story of the Parisian underworld, in which Warner played an American in love with a café dancer who had a very disagreeable Apache lover. Here for the first time, Warner Baxter's name took the most important place in the billing. He followed this rather unimportant presentation with an excellent performance in "Craig's Wife," the story of a selfish wife who valued the neatness of her home above the comfort and happiness of her husband and so lost him. The theme lacked the immediate drama necessary to satisfy the motion picture, but it was an interesting and well acted picture, nevertheless.

78

The next film in which he appeared was "Ramona," a beautiful, slow-moving screen version of the novel by Helen Hunt Jackson. Warner's rôle was that of Alessandro, the Indian lover whom Ramona marries. Their tragedy was swift and complete: their child dies—for lack of care, their home is burned and their lands laid waste; finally Alessandro is shot down in cold blood and Ramona goes mad. Warner's rôle was necessarily static, until the last reels, but he played it with dignity and restrained emotion. "West of Zanzibar," which followed, was a lurid melodrama of jungle life and unpleasant affairs, taken from the play "Congo." Here he played the part of a once respectable doctor gone to seed, the victim of an evil man, who was driven half insane by his lust for revenge. The last film he made that year was "Dan-

79

ger Street," an underworld melodrama based on "The Beautiful Bullet," by Harold MacGrath.

The following year, 1929, was to bring about many changes in the position held by Warner Baxter on the screen. First of all, it was the year in which talking films first became a serious problem, and those actors possessed of good speaking voices found themselves in a position to ask almost anything that they wanted. No one knew much about Warner's voice, however, and since his pictures had not, of late, been anything out of the ordinary, no one troubled to find out about it—that is, no one except William Fox. This enterprising producer, faced with the necessity of making talking films, decided that for his first feature picture he would take O. Henry's brilliantly ironic short story, "The Caballero's Way,"

Warner Baxter

and turn it into an all-talking out-door picture. It was a daring experiment, for nothing of that sort had ever been tried before, but Mr. Fox apparently felt that since he was taking the plunge with sound, he might as well go still further and include nature. For the three leading parts he selected Warner Baxter to play the title rôle, Edmund Lowe for Sergeant Mickey Dunn, and Dorothy Burgess for Tonia Maria, the faithless Mexican girl who played one lover against another.

This selection of players was brilliantly successful, and Warner Baxter's performance was nothing short of a triumph. Something in the rôle of the glamorous 'Cisco Kid, who played Robin Hood on the outskirts of the Mojave Desert, seemed to tap hitherto unsuspected springs of achievement in Warner. His easy carriage, his grace, his vibrant, sonorous voice, which made broken English sound like a new language, above all his sense of the romantic and picturesque, caused audiences and producers all over the country to sit up and wonder where so brilliant and beguiling an actor had been keeping himself all this time. The picture was not only a complete vindication of talking films, but also of Warner Baxter, for any player who could be both romantic and loquacious at the same time was a veritable gift of the gods. As the irresistible bandit who could love, steal, and avenge himself without hate, Warner Baxter was the living embodiment of hitherto impalpable illusions; gay, charming, lovable, and marvelously convincing.

During the months that followed he played in a diversity of rôles: a triple and extremely interesting part in "Through Different Eyes," which was a murder mystery with really novel twists, "Behind That Curtain," another mystery story, "The Far Call," and "Romance of the Rio Grande." The last named was an effort to capitalize somewhat the success of "In Old Arizona" by giving Mr. Baxter a chance to dress up in Spanish costume once more, have various exciting adventures, and make love to at least three beautiful ladies. It was an entertaining film, pleasing to the eye, and very well acted, but it suffered in places from a lack of coherence. The star was handsome and soulful, the assorted heroines duly charming, but the effect was blurred by the omission of a consistent plot and logical continuity. Next to "In Old Arizona," however, it was the most popular picture in which Warner Baxter appeared that season.

The next year an effort was made by Fox Films, to which organization he had been under contract since his notably successful screen debut, to maintain Warner as a romantic actor and at the same time to vary his rôles. Accordingly, he played in a short film, "Happy Days," a get-together party of all the players in the company, and was then cast for the leading parts in "Such Men Are Dangerous," and "The Arizona Kid." The first of the two latter was one of Elinor Glyn's highly colored and improbable romances about a fabulously rich and ugly man whose bride leaves him on account of his lack of soul. Pretending to be dead, he has his face recast and then sets out to woo her in his new guise. It was obviously a freak part, and Mr. Baxter, frequently ill at ease in its absurdities, did all that was possible, first to make himself hideous, then to be handsome and debonair. He was more successful, needless to say, in the latter guise. The film was the indirect cause of a regrettable tragedy, when two aeroplanes, engaged in filming a leap into the ocean, met in midair with the loss of ten lives.

"The Arizona Kid" found Warner back on safer and pleasanter ground, playing his former successful part, that of the romantic bandit. He has managed to make this rôle his own to an extraordinary degree. The actor's voice, carriage, face and bearing, the ease with which he bestrides a horse, the nonchalant manner in which he does his killing, and his complete identification with the character of the colorful desperado, all combine to make it his best part. Particularly noteworthy is the fact that he can lay claim to being the only actor now appearing in talking films who is able to speak that peculiar combination of Spanish and English always associated with bandits and still remain attractive. In "Renegades," his third important film for the year, he was not so fortunately situated. The story is a very melodramatic conception of four men, all with questionable pasts, who enlist in the Foreign Legion, desert to the Arabs, and are finally killed in an endeavor to save their former comrades in arms. Mr. Baxter, as the ringleader, struggled valiantly to make the character's sudden change of mood plausible and sympathetic, but it was a lost cause.

Later films in which he appeared are "Doctors' Wives," "Their Mad Moment," "The Squaw Man," and "Daddy-Long-Legs," the latter with Janet Gaynor. "Doctors' Wives," an attempt to make a romantic figure out of a realistic one, was not altogether a good choice. Warner played a handsome doctor whose jealous wife suspected him of making love to all his attractive patients, and while he gave a very sincere and earnest performance, it was not the sort of rôle in which he is seen to best advantage, being but meagerly defined, and depicting a type rather than a character. "Their Mad Moment," taken from Eleanor Mercein's novel, "Basquerie," is the romance of a proud young Basque and a spoiled American girl; it offers the sort of rôle which Mr. Baxter prefers, presenting opportunities for romantic love making. "The Squaw Man," taken from the celebrated stage play, unfolds the story of a British nobleman who, taking on himself the disgrace rightfully incurred by his brother, comes to America and marries an

Indian woman, only to be restored to his rightful station in the end. This film, produced by United Artists, was the first of his films in many months which had not been made by Fox. In "Daddy-Long-Legs" he played the title rôle, appearing as a handsome young bachelor who adopts a plucky little orphan with whom he is later on to fall in love. His most recent pictures are "The 'Cisco Kid," in which he once more assumes the romantic guise of O. Henry's lovable bandit, first played by him in "In Old Arizona," and "Surrender."

When he is not acting on the screen—and of late this is seldom—Warner Baxter finds various pastimes to amuse him. He plays tennis and even undertook to learn the Basque game of pelota to add verisimilitude to the character he was portraying in "Their Mad Moment." Hunting is another of his favorite sports. He owns a cabin in the San Jacinto Mountains, the walls of which are covered with the pelts of foxes that he has trapped during the winter months. His idiosyncrasies range from great fastidiousness in clothes to his insistence upon driving his own car, even though he has a chauffeur. Everything in his home must be in its right place, and he makes certain that this state of neatness shall prevail by waiting on himself on every possible occasion.

As has been proved by many other famous actors, height is no criterion of acting ability. Warner Baxter is under six feet in height, though he looks tall on the screen, yet he can put more active charm, more convincing romance and more glamor into his playing than any two or three stars whom you might choose to name. It may be true that the films will win their greatest achievements in the realm of realism, but so long as there are players of Warner Baxter's caliber, romance—not just sweet sentiment—is bound to retain abounding popularity.

CHARLES CHAPLIN

To TELL the life story of Charles Spencer Chaplin, the "Charlie," or "Charlot," of so many millions, is almost like attempting to give the history of the motion picture industry from its beginnings. He has been part of the film world for so many years that one feels that he must have been there always: it is inconceivable to think of motion pictures without him. Even when, as now, he turns out but one film in three years, he still remains the object of intense interest and curiosity. By nature small and slender with deep blue eyes, and hair that is rapidly turning gray, on the screen he is the immortal, comic, and pathetic little tramp, with the derby hat, the shock of black hair, the little moustache, the tight little coat, the enormous trousers, the oversize shoes, and the jaunty cane. He wears perpetually the air of an optimistic mongrel puppy, left out in the rain too long, rather bedraggled in appearance, and desperately anxious for a bit of kindness and affection. In private life he dresses with neatness and in style; his clothes only call attention to him because of their excellent cut. Like most comedians, he is moody, often depressed, and not always sure of what he wants. Once he gets an idea into his mind, however, he works it to the full with all his tremendous energy.

From the time of his start in motion pictures, back in 1913, he has never varied his style of costuming, or of make-up. Invariably, he plays the little tramp, and each picture is, while complete in itself, but another chapter in the Odyssey of this strangely universal specimen of humanity. His

92

films have but little plot, depending for their effect on the fertile brain of their protagonist. People use all sorts of adjectives to describe his fascination, but it all boils down to a few simple phrases,—he makes you laugh, he makes you cry, he makes you do both at once; you see the comic and the tragic aspects of what without him would be dull, routine, everyday life. Consciously or unconsciously, gaily or sadly, he has created a figure that will never be forgotten, personifying, perhaps, our futile, groping, and appealingly comic inner selves—so well intentioned and so incapable of fulfillment.

Charlie was born in London on April 16, 1889. His parents were not well off, and the little boy grew up in the atmosphere of the English music halls, where his father earned a living as actor and singer. The elder Chaplin, also named Charlie, was

93

known for his ability to play a great variety
of parts and also for his knowledge of music.
Mrs. Chaplin gained something of a reputation as a singer in Gilbert and Sullivan
operettas, and it was during one of her engagements at a leading variety theatre that
Charlie was born. He made his first appearance on any stage as a baby in his mother's arms. It is pleasant to know that she
lived long enough to enjoy the enormous
fame and popularity of her son: she died in
August, 1928, at Beverly Hills, California.

While Charlie was still a young child, his
father died, and when the boy was old
enough, he turned to the stage as the most
natural way of earning a livelihood. His
first engagement was with a group of juvenile dancers, known as the "Eight Lancashire
Lads." His most celebrated part in those
early days was as the page boy, Billy, in

"Sherlock Holmes," in the company in which Beerbohm Tree was playing the title rôle. Being a somewhat precocious child and a keen observer of the idiosyncrasies of others, he took to imitating Mr. Tree, and other members of the cast, with the result that he found himself quite in demand as an impersonator, and was frequently invited to entertain at actors' clubs. This employment was uncertain at best, and when the run of the play came to an end, Charlie was hard up. He tried to win a guinea offered to the winner of an amateur clogging contest in a local music hall, but the manager recognized him as one of the "'Eight Lancashire Lads" and ejected him from the theatre.

About this time he attracted the attention of Arthur Reeves, the American manager of Karno's "Mumming Birds," a variety turn which toured the English music halls and in which Charlie's brother, Sidney, was taking part. Fred Karno consented to his quest to allow Charlie to go to America in the company then being assembled. Accordingly, Charlie Chaplin made his first appearance in the United States playing the rôle of a drunken "swell" in the sketch entitled, "A Night in a London Music Hall." His salary was then ten dollars a week. The company traveled extensively in the United States and Canada until the spring of 1912, when bookings in England forced them to return home. None the less, the autumn of that same year found them playing return engagements.

By this time, Charlie had begun to attract attention, and he received an offer from the Keystone Film Company to make pictures for a year at a salary of one hundred and fifty dollars a week. He accepted this contract, but remained with the English company until the tour came to an end in Kansas City, leaving him free to go to Hollywood.

With his entrance into films, Charlie began his embodiment of the famous little tramp, a guise which he has continued, substantially without alteration, up to the present time. Questioned as to where he found this quaint character, Charlie explained that the unique walk had been suggested by an old London cab-driver, and that the big shoes, indicating enormous flat feet, were suggested by a comedian whom he had once seen. The rest of the make-up he had evolved himself. Charlie's fame spread abroad with the launching of "The Champion," the first of the Keystone comedies, in which he took the part of a desperate little man who knocks out a much larger opponent by putting a horse-shoe in his glove.

Many others followed; among them were "A Day's Pleasure," "Making a Living," "Dough and Dynamite," "Tillie's Punctured Romance," (with Marie Dressler), "The Piano Movers," "Charlie At Work," "Charlie the Tramp," "The Kids' Auto Races," "The Property Man," "The Perfect Lady," "Charlie by the Sea," "Charlie at the Show," and "Police." One of the most famous of these was "Tillie's Punctured Romance," a full length comedy, undertaken by Charlie and Marie Dressler on their own initiative and considered a very daring experiment.

Following his work with Keystone, Charlie went to the Essenay Studios, where he appeared in "The Plumber," "A Night in the Show," "The Stage," "His New Job," "The Bank," "A Night Out," "In the Park," "The Jitney Elopement," "Shanghaied," and the famous burlesque on "Carmen" in which he was assisted by Marie Dressler. With the every-increasing circulation of these films, Charlie's popularity and fame grew by leaps and bounds. His next venture was with Mutual Pictures, and for them he made "The Floorwalker," "The Adventurer," "One A. M.," "The Pawnshop," "The Cure," "The Fireman," "The Ring," "The Immigrant," and "The Count." The greater his reputation, the more ambitious were his films.

In 1917 he signed a contract with First National Pictures and released through that organization a number of pictures that have become famous all over the world. Among these will be found "A Dog's Life," "Shoulder Arms," "Sunnyside," "The Idle Class," "Pay Day," "The Kid" and "The Pilgrim." Audiences today find these films just as

laughable and pathetic, as when they were
first released. Everyone has his own favor-
ites among Charlie's films; for in each one
of them there are episodes to remember
because their conception and execution
verged on genius. From "The Pilgrim"
there is the marvelous sermon on David and
Goliath, (preached entirely in pantomime),
and Charlie's surreptitious administering
of chastisement to the insufferable small
boy. From "The Kid," one recalls the tiny
little youngster, toddling anxiously down
the road after the diminutive figure of his
friend and protector, the forlorn tramp.
This youngster, Jackie Coogan, can justly
rank as the greatest of Charlie Chaplin's
discoveries, and the two of them—man and
boy—were responsible for the overwhelming success of the picture. In "Shoulder
Arms," Charlie suffers grotesquely and un-

complainingly the horrors of drill sergeants and the discomforts of sleeping in three feet of water. Innumerable other episodes might be quoted, but these suffice.

It was hardly to be expected that Charlie's fame could be confined within the borders of this country. Indeed, his films circulated throughout Europe, Asia and even Africa; and on the Continent he was being hailed as a genius long before persons in this country had stopped thinking of him as anything but a slap-stick comedian. Europe has always been more interested in the art of pantomime than have the English-speaking countries, and Charlie's gestures, so painstakingly and graphically developed, were appreciated more abroad than here. None the less, his marvelous combination of the wildest fun-making and the infinite pathos of the down-trodden members of society, gradually began to attract universal attention. Wide-awake Americans brought home stories of how Paris went mad about "Charlot," how they discussed his every motion and analyzed each lift of his eyebrow, and presently a sort of Chaplin cult began to spread in this country. Everything that he turned out was expected to be a work of the most supreme genius, and if Charlie chanced to nod, as the finest of artists will, it became almost a national calamity.

By 1918, Charlie Chaplin decided to launch out for himself. His films were still to be released through First National Pictures, but his was to be the sole voice in selection of cast and stories, as well as in the matter of direction. One of the most famous films he ever made was "A Woman of Paris,"—the only production in which he did not appear himself. It introduced

Adolphe Menjou in the rôle of the charming, worldly wise, sophisticated gentleman
which he was later to make so famous: also
it proved that a worn-out theme—the
eternal triangle—could be handled with
such delicacy and skill as to give to it a new
freshness and an absorbing interest. Many
thought that Charlie would give up acting
for directing and producing alone, when
faced with the great artistic success of "A
Woman of Paris," but it was only in the
nature of an experiment, and he soon returned to the screen in person.

Two years after organizing his own company, Charlie Chaplin joined forces with
Douglas Fairbanks, Mary Pickford, and
D. W. Griffith to form the United Artists
Corporation, an organization now compris-
ing many of the foremost stars and producers in the motion picture industry. The

intention of its originators was primarily to secure that independence in filmdom which Charlie has always championed. When an attempt was made not long afterwards to merge United Artists with Metro-Goldwyn-Mayer, Charlie opposed it so strenuously that the idea was abandoned. Through United Artists, Charlie has released "The Gold Rush," "The Circus" and "City Lights."

"The Gold Rush," shown for the first time in September, 1925, may well stand at the top of the list of all Charlie's productions. It was very elaborate, marvelously conceived, and carried out without a suggestion of over-planning or sophistication. It also ranks among the infinitesimally small number of Chaplin films which bring the hero a happiness and fabulous wealth. There are many episodes which come to mind: the dance which Charlie executes with two forks and a couple of dinner rolls; his attempt to cook and eat one of his enormous shoes; the wild moment in which the gigantic hairy trapper mistakes Charlie for a huge chicken and tries to carve him. "The Circus" furnished Charlie's wild bicycle ride on the tight-rope, with his safety-belt dangling above his head, and the monkeys biting his ear. On the whole, "The Circus" was not quite up to its predecessor, being a shade too carefully contrived, but those who saw it will not soon forget it.

"The Circus" was released in 1928, and a few months after its successful launching, Charlie announced that his next picture would be called "City Lights." Work began on this film shortly and was carried on, with frequent interruptions, until the first public showing on February 1, 1931, in Los

Angeles. Those three years saw more changes in motion pictures than one would believe possible: the coming of sound effects and speech had veritably revolutionized the industry. Yet when "City Lights" was presented to the public, it became apparent that Charlie had not changed. Steadfastly, he had set his face against talking films, and despite the dismal predictions of what would befall a silent picture, he refused to introduce dialogue into "City Lights." To be sure, there is sound in the delicious burlesque of talking films which opens the picture, also in the marvelous episode of the swallowed whistle, and all the multifarious noises of the city itself, but not a word is actually spoken. So long as he appears on the screen as the little tramp, Charlie will not open his mouth, to do so would mean the destruction of the figure that has

106

required years of study and insight to build. The little tramp does not need to talk; his language is universal and, therefore, needs no translation; his enormous popularity springs from the fact that his actions are as easily understood in Japan as in New York. Should Charlie launch forth into making the life of Napoleon—a project which he has cherished for years—he might be willing to speak. Just at present, however, his silence is worth far more to him than any speech could be, in proof of which he refused an enormous offer made to him by a big broadcasting company just before he left on his triumphal tour of Europe. "City Lights," for all its synchronized score—composed by Charlie himself—offers little change from his earlier productions, and, the enthusiasm with which it was received, proves that people will accept Charlie in silent films as long as he cares to make them.

The Charlie Chaplin of the screen and the Charles Spencer Chaplin, whom great countries honor, and whose name appears in the headlines for a variety of reasons, are curiously different persons. In films, Charlie plays a down-trodden, abused and optimistic waif. In real life, he is a hard-headed, intelligent business man, who spends money in order to make more, and who can drive extraordinary bargains with those who wish to show his films. He has been decorated by the French government with the Legion of Honor; he has also been involved in two divorce suits of great length and unpleasantness. His first marriage, to Mildred Harris, was contracted in 1918 and ended two years later in the divorce courts. Six years later, after he had been reported engaged to any number of prominent screen

Charles Chaplin

actresses, he eloped to Mexico and married his sixteen-year-old leading lady, Lita Gray. There were two children, Charles Spencer Chaplin, Jr., born on June 27, 1925, and Sidney Earle Chaplin, born on March 30, 1926. Unfortunately, this second marriage did not last and in the late autumn of 1926, Mrs. Chaplin sued for divorce. The suit dragged endlessly along until the summer of 1928, when the decree was made final and Mrs. Chaplin received the custody of the two children.

Charlie Chaplin is an unpredictable personage, and his ideas can never be foreseen. In the year 1925, he seriously considered building a costly theatre in New York and becoming a playwright, producer, manager and actor. He even went so far as to approach Judith Anderson—whose acting in "The Dove" had greatly impressed him—

109

with the suggestion that she become his leading lady. Nothing came of this, however. The same year an even more interesting episode took place. He sued an actor, named Charles Amado, for imitating his mannerisms, copying his comedy business, and employing the stage name of Charles Aplin. The case was argued back and forth for weeks and aroused much interested discussion over how far an actor could retain the exclusive rights to a particular brand of comedy. Charlie won the suit and has no further reason to fear further plagiarisms.

Only very infrequently does Charlie consent to analyze the character which he has made so justly famous. Then, as was evident in a recent interview, he deals in generalities and talks of the universal aspects of down-trodden humanity and his wish to embody this stratum of society in a single figure. This means but little, however, to those to whom Charlie appeals: they wish to be entertained and are not interested in grandiloquent phraseology. Realizing this, Charlie is content to let others analyze his technique and discuss the reasons for his popularity. Enough for him that he makes his pictures well, and that the public is satisfied that he is the supreme comedian of our time.

MAURICE CHEVALIER

SEEN on the screen, Maurice Chevalier
is the very embodiment of debonair joy-
ousness, lighthearted pleasure, and carefree
success. Off the screen, he might not be
recognized as the same man. Allowed to
relax for a moment, permitted to drop the
gaily humorous aspect, he appears a quiet,
often somber, possibly cynical personage.
He is in truth a man with two masks: one
for the public, and one for himself. If this
were not so, it would be surprising, for
Chevalier's life has been difficult, tragic,
filled with moments when success and failure hung in the balance. A life which in-
cludes a childhood in the direst poverty,
three years in a German prison camp after

a wound that had supposedly crippled his singing powers forever, a failure in his first attempt to win a place in the Paris music halls, and a near failure in his first American talking picture. Sickness, uncertainty, discouragement, and deferred hope hardly seem the proper background for so gay and enchanting a personality as Maurice Chevalier, idolized in his native land, tremendously popular in the United States. That he gives us always the bright and never the dark side of his nature, shows the courage and spirit that went into his makeup.

Maurice Chevalier was born in Menilmontant, that quarter of Paris corresponding to Whitechapel in London or the Lower East Side of New York, though said to be less desirable than either. The day of his birth was September twelfth, but the year is uncertain: presumably it was about 1895, for he began his military service in 1913 and previously had been on the stage for two or three years. The family were terribly poor: his father was a house-painter and when trade was bad, Mme. Chevalier worked as a charwoman. Maurice was always her favorite son, and it is pleasant to know that she lived long enough to share in his prosperity after working so hard for him in the preceding years. So bitter was the poverty in which the boy grew up that the ultimate goal of his dreams was a spending allowance of one franc a week. He was scarcely more than a young child when he had to work to supplement his parents' scanty earnings. All sorts of jobs were tried: he worked for a joiner, acted as chandler's boy, and was apprentice in a nail factory. None of them suited him, and from each one he was very soon discharged.

Not that he was a bad boy: it was simply that almost from infancy, he was determined to become an actor. At the age of eleven years, he announced that he was going on the stage. This precipitated a terrible scene at home, for his family could see no future in it and thought that he would be just a good-for-nothing. His start, when it finally came, was on a very small scale: the manager of a cheap café hired him for a few francs a week to sing comic songs. Much to his sorrow, he did not begin to attain normal height until he was sixteen years of age. Owing to his undersized body, he was billed as "The Midget Comedian." This café singing led to a small engagement in a boulevard theatre which was followed by another turn at a suburban music hall, the scene of his first success.

During this difficult period he was aided

materially by two men—J. W. Jackson, an English entertainer, and Norman French, an American dancer. From Jackson, Chevalier learned English music hall technique and stage dancing; from French, who was a tremendous favorite of the day, he acquired the type of modern eccentric dancing which he still uses. At Jackson's suggestion, Chevalier used to make trips to London at intervals of several months, to study what was going on in the English Theatre, particularly in the musical comedy line. At the same time, he was working day and night to improve his dancing and perfect his technique. When the great opportunity came he was ready for it. He was offered an engagement at the famous Folies Bergere where Mistinguett, idol of the halls, was playing. In one dance number Chevalier served as her partner and won her instant approval. To continue as her dancing partner, a position which was soon offered him, he was also obliged to demonstrate his fistic ability to another aspirant behind the theatre. Fortunately for him he was able to defend his hard won position.

At last his prospects appeared brilliant, but the war clouds over Europe were threatening and men were needed for more harrowing careers than singing and dancing. Chevalier had begun his compulsory military service in 1913 and before his term was over, war was declared. His regiment was sent directly into the firing lines, where he saw brief and bloody service. After conducting himself with the utmost bravery, during a German attack at Cutry, he was struck down by a fragment of shell which pierced his lung. He recovered consciousness in a German hospital, and for the next

two years he remained in a prison camp at
Alten Grabow near Magdeburg, Germany.
One of his intimates at this time was an
English soldier, Ronald Kennedy, from
whom Chevalier learned to speak the English language. Their friendship endures
to this day. His damaged lung caused him
untold suffering, and the German doctors
warned him that he could never sing again.
None the less he managed to keep up his
spirits and those of his fellow prisoners
by organizing concerts and entertainments
which so won him the favor of the German
officials that he soon gained the freedom
of the camp. Chevalier was, like all prisoners, anxious to get back to France. One
evening, in company with another French
soldier, he made his escape, walking out
of Alten Grabow in the disguise of a German field-hospital attendant.

Arriving safely in France, after many adventures, Chevalier found himself invalided to Paris, for his wound did not permit of further military service. Not knowing what else to do, he tried to pick up the old life where he had left it to go to war, but his former confidence was gone. He obtained an engagement at a music hall where he had sung before, and though the audience greeted him with the utmost enthusiasm, he left the stage trembling and with the tears running down his face. He did not feel that he could possibly go on. At this crucial moment, however, an event occurred which restored his lost faith and gave him the inspiration to carry on. When he reached his dressing room he found a letter from the French government informing him that he had been decorated with the Croix de Guerre for his gallant conduct at Cutry.

With this encouragement he dared to banish his own fears and proved the doctors had been wrong. Up to this time, he had always appeared as a grotesque comedian with ludicrous makeup and preposterous clothes, but now he came to the conclusion was the time to make a change. From what he had seen of English music hall work and the assurance of American stage dancers and comedians, he realized that it was necessary to charm an audience as well as to amuse them. With this in mind he evolved the appearance with which Europe and America are now familiar: the dinner coat and the straw hat, cocked at a jaunty and rakish angle over one eye. It was an innovation which worked like magic. His fame spread across the English channel where it reached the ears of Elsie Janis, just arrived in London to star in "Hello, America" for Sir Alfred Butt. She urged, then insisted, that Chevalier be brought to England to play with her, and at last she won her point. Chevalier came, suffered badly from stage-fright, but thanks to the encouragement of Miss Janis, soon recovered his poise.

With "Hello, America" behind him as a solid success, Chevalier returned to France to continue his career. Once more paired with the tremendously popular Mistinguett, he became the most popular stage figure in the French capital, in his field. The idols of the town they remained for many months. Presently they became too prominent to play together any more, and accordingly separated, but each continued to be as successful alone. Chevalier again went to London, this time with assurance unmixed with timidity, where he played in

"White Birds," a revue produced at His Majesty's Theatre on May 31, 1927. With him came a charming little singer and actress, Yvonne Vallee, whom he was shortly afterwards to marry. They achieved success in the revue and were well spoken of, though the entertainment itself did not last over long. Returning to Paris, Chevalier went to the Casino de Paris where in company with Mlle. Vallee he starred in a great success. His songs became widely known throughout Europe and he soon achieved that pinnacle of fame where others could earn money by imitating him.

Talking pictures were soon to lure him across the Atlantic, although he had been unwilling to risk his reputation in the silent screen, feeling that silence would put an insuperable barrier between him and audiences not composed of his own countrymen.

Early in 1928, Jesse L. Lasky, first vice-president in charge of production for Paramount, made a special trip to Paris to obtain Chevalier's consent to a contract to make films in this country. Realizing that with the added advantages of sound, he would stand a far better chance, Chevalier accepted the Paramount offer, and by August of that year he was in Hollywood ready to begin work.

The first film that he made was "The Innocents of Paris," in which he worked under the direction of Richard Wallace. The picture did not take long to produce and was soon released. Curiously enough, "The Innocents of Paris" (an unlikely and over-sentimentalized story), was but cooly received in the larger cities, where it might have been expected that Chevalier's name was sufficient to insure its success.

Somewhat discouraged, Chevalier went back to Paris for a holiday, while the studio took stock of the returns from the film. It has often been said that although a film may succeed in the big cities failure in the smaller districts which send in the biggest returns, casts the deciding vote. Such was the case with "The Innocents of Paris," which proved tremendously popular all over the country. Telegrams were hastily despatched for Chevalier to come back at once and make more pictures. Meantime, he was having a splendid time in France, where he found himself even more popular than before he left. So great was the demand to see him that for an engagement of brief duration at the Empire music hall he was paid 15,000 francs a week, an unheard-of sum for Paris. Followed by many regrets, he set sail once more for the

124

United States to fulfill the obligations of his contract.

In his second picture, Chevalier fared better. Instead of the sentimental banalities of a fictitious Paris underworld, he was given a gay mingling of comedy, drama, and romance, presented in a delightful musical setting. This was the famous "Love Parade" which proved so signal a triumph for everyone connected with it: for Chevalier, for Jeanette MacDonald, in the leading feminine rôle, for Ernst Lubitsch, the director, and for Paramount. It was a gay, sophisticated story of a handsome young officer who marries a beautiful young queen and then finds that being the queen's husband is something less than a man-sized job. Chevalier was truly in his element as the spruce officer whose reputation with the ladies won him first the annoyance, then the curiosity, and finally the love of the royal lady. The film was a great success and definitely established Chevalier as a popular star of the first magnitude.

Not all his time, however, was devoted to the screen, for on February 18, 1929, he made his American stage debut in the Ziegfeld Midnight Frolic on the roof of the New Amsterdam Theatre in New York. Audiences responded to him immediately, finding his pronounced French accent no barrier to their enjoyment. His expansive good humor, his brilliant and infectious smile won the hearts of those who saw him before he had a chance to speak a word. The dynamic quality of his personality, his bubbling good humor, and his completely individual method of putting over his songs, carried all before them.

Admittedly, "The Love Parade" set a

126

Maurice Chevalier

standard so high that almost any other picture would suffer in comparison. None the
less, it must be admitted that those films
which followed, "The Big Pond," and "The
Playboy of Paris," were hardly good
enough for their chief performer. The
first was a light comedy in which a French-
man proves himself as good a business man
as the best of his American competitors,
and the second dealt with a waiter in a
French café who inherits a fortune but finds
himself bound by a semi-fraudulent contract to either continue in his menial position or else forfeit a good half of his money.
There was singing in each film, and two
song hits from "The Big Pond"—"My
Ideal" and "You Brought a New Kind of
Love to Me"—have spread all over the
country. None the less, the plots were very
thin indeed and made pitifully little use

of those talents which Chevalier had revealed so abundantly in "The Love Parade." A return to the style of this successful piece is made in "The Smiling Lieutenant," a comedy drama interpolated with a number of songs. The public likes to hear him sing, clamors for him to sing, in fact, and although musical films are waning in popularity, Chevalier continues to warble quite as happily and successfully as he formerly did in the Paris music halls.

While the nature of his work keeps him indoors much of the time, Chevalier has a distinct preference for an out-of-door life. His favorite sport is boxing, in which he is both an authority and an expert. He has often sparred with Georges Carpentier, a friend of many years' standing. He makes no pretense of grace or beauty, nor does his deficiency in these attributes appear to bother him. If you have ever chanced to observe his walk closely, you will find that his legs are those of a veteran cavalry officer. Indeed, one might venture the suggestion that he was built originally to go with a horse. He is very fond of golf, and swims well enough to enjoy himself immensely. He is so slight that he does not give the impression of height, yet he is six feet tall. His eyes are blue, his hair smooth and brown, his complexion ruddy and his build athletic. He believes in moderation in all things, and eats sparingly, preferably of French food.

At the studio his work is not limited entirely to films for American screens, as he has appeared in French versions of "The Big Pond" and "The Playboy of Paris." These pictures, released under the titles of "Le Grand Mare" and "Le Petit Café," have been shown on both sides of the Atlantic. One might say that Chevalier seems a trifle more at ease in the French dialogue versions than in the English, yet the difference is slight, the spectator is chiefly conscious that the actor is a trifle freer in his own tongue, when he does not need to worry about the pronunciation of what is, after all, a foreign language. Aside from these pictures, he appeared in "Paramount on Parade."

The popularity of Maurice Chevalier appears to be steadily on the up-grade. No one will maintain that he is a great actor, but he is something equally popular: a distinct and charming personality. Certain mannerisms, certain inflections that he uses may be imitations, but no mimic can set before you the man himself. To define his charm would require an exhaustive analysis of his singing voice, a discussion of the pleasure one takes in that all-embracing smile, and a detailed exposition of the reasons why it is so much more agreeable to hear this actor mispronounce English than to listen to others speak it without flaw and without sparkle. Chevalier is a world of entertainment because he is himself; not because he possesses certain very definite assets, but because there is something about him that makes you like him.

RONALD COLMAN

ALL the world loves a mystery, particularly an attractive one. This helps to explain in part the fascination Ronald Colman has exerted over the feminine motion picture public ever since he blossomed out as a full-fledged romantic actor in support of Lillian Gish in "The White Sister." Talking films have changed him somewhat since then, giving him the chance to develop his talents for light comedy at the expense of some of the more serious aspects of his acting. None the less, audible or silent, he remains polite, distant, and impenetrable; by his refusal to live in the quiet privacy of the goldfish bowl of Hollywood's limelight, he has shrouded himself in a veil of mystery, and nourished that priceless attribute, romantic illusion, without which there could be no motion picture industry. Apparently, all this has been accomplished without conscious effort on his part. On the screen he belongs to the public; off the screen he feels that he has the right to belong to himself.

He has had an active, often dangerous, and frequently exciting career, and the road he has had to travel to his present comfortable position in filmdom was by no means easy, even for a young man with his personal attractions and undoubted histrionic talent. Ronald was born at Richmond, in Surrey, England, on February 9, 1891. His father was Charles Colman, a silk importer, and his mother the former Marjory Fraser. Up to the time that he was sixteen, he attended the Hadley School at Littlehampton, Sussex, but his school days were brought to an abrupt end by the death of his father in 1907. The state of the family income did not permit of further study, so that Ronald was obliged to go to work immediately. His first job was as office boy for the Britain Steamship Company in London at a truly munificent salary equivalent to about $2.50 a week. He remained with this company for five years, becoming in turn bookkeeper and then junior accountant.

His fondness for acting dates back to his school days, and not even bookkeeping could discourage it. While still in school he had taken part in amateur theatricals, acting in such plays as "The Admirable Crichton," "Sowing the Wind," and "Fanny's First Play." While in London he joined the Bancroft Amateur Dramatic Society for the sake of keeping his hand in, and at the same time, for exercise and diversion, he joined the London Scottish Regiment. This organization, somewhat similar to the National Guard in this country, kept him busy until 1913 when his enlistment came to an end. The playing at soldiering, however, was but the prelude to something far more serious, for when war was declared on August 4, 1914, Ronald promptly gave up his position to reenlist in his old regiment.

This regiment formed a part of Lord Kitchener's First Hundred Thousand and was among the foremost to go to France. By September of that year Ronald was serving in France as a private soldier in the Old Contemptibles of glorious memory. He saw service in the front line trenches in the first battle of Ypres and had the decidedly unpleasant experience of being

135

buried alive by the explosion of a shell. Dug out unharmed, he soon met with an accident that brought his career in active service to an end. He had been sent with his company to reinforce the troops in the front line trenches by Messines Ridge. On the way a shell, exploding nearby, caused him to stumble and fracture his ankle so badly that he was unable to continue with his regiment. He spent his second year in the army back in England attached to the Highland Brigade doing clerical work. Not satisfied with this, he made numerous attempts to get back into action with other branches of the army, but early in 1916 the medical board discharged him as incapacitated for further service.

Debarred from serving his country on the firing line, Ronald went back to his first love, the theatrical world, obtaining his first regular engagement with Lena Ashwell during the summer of 1916. His debut on the professional stage was made in "The Maharanee of Arakan," a playlet written for Miss Ashwell by Rabindranath Tagore and presented by her at the Coliseum in London. Ronald played a herald—and played him, if you please, in blackface! His next part, somewhat more important, was in support of Gladys Cooper in "The Misleading Lady." After that came a leading rôle in "Damaged Goods," and his first offer to go on the screen. George Dewhurst, a British film producer, offered him the chance to play in a two-reel comedy that was photographed in an improvised studio rigged up in a vacant house. Sad to relate, this picture was never released, so no one can tell what Ronald looked like on the occasion of his screen debut: that is, no one but Ronald himself, and he is not likely to give out that information. In spite of this bad beginning, Ronald continued to make pictures for the next three years, among them "Snow in the Desert," and "The Black Spider." At one time he was asked to play a Jewish pugilist in "A Son of David," who had, like his famous namesake, to knock out a much bigger man than himself.

Despite this dazzling offer, Ronald continued to play on the stage, for he had a very poor opinion of himself as a screen player. He achieved considerable success in the theatre and acted important rôles in "The Live Wire," "The Great Day," and "The Little Brother." Just when it seemed that he had really established himself on the British stage, there came the great depression of 1920, and Ronald found himself

138

unable to obtain steady work as an actor. Deciding that the prospects at home were bad and likely to remain so, Ronald packed his bag and came to the United States. When he arrived in New York in the autumn of 1920 his stock of worldly goods consisted of the sum of thirty-seven dollars, three clean collars, and two letters of introduction. To save money, he lived in a cheap furnished room in Brooklyn, while day after day, in desperation, he toured the motion picture studios and theatrical managers' offices in search of work. He was down to his last dollar when he finally obtained a part in support of Robert Warwick in "The Dauntless Three." The play did not last long, but it offered Ronald two separate and distinct parts. In the first act he played the chief of the Turkish police, and in Act Two, made his appearance as a Russian spy with a very impressive beard. After that, work was not quite so difficult to obtain. Among other plays in which he appeared were "The Night Cap," "The Silver Fox," "East Is West," and "The Green Goddess," in which he supported George Arliss, playing the part of a temple priest.

His opportunity came during the following autumn when he was engaged to support Henry Miller and Ruth Chatterton in Henri Bataille's "La Tendresse." The play dealt with the relationship of a middle-aged French playwright and his beautiful mistress who is betraying him for a younger man. Ronald took the rôle of the youthful lover, Alain Sergyll, and handled it so beautifully that Henry King, then collecting a cast to support Lillian Gish in "The White Sister," saw in him the ideal choice for the leading male rôle. Thus Ronald made his

first bid for fame in the motion picture
world. The company of "The White Sister" went to Italy, where the film was to
be photographed, and Ronald soon convinced Mr. King that he had made no mistake. The story, taken from a novel by F.
Marion Crawford, told how a young Italian
girl, believing that her soldier lover has
been killed in battle with the Arabs, becomes a nun, taking her final vows just
before he escapes and returns to marry her.
In the part of the handsome, desperate
young lover, so attractive in his uniform
that it was no wonder all the ladies in the
cast were supposed to be in love with him,
Ronald succeeded in dominating the film
every moment that he appeared before the
camera. The picture was beautifully photographed, finely acted and, somewhat sur-
prisingly, endowed with an unhappy end-

141

ing in which the hero gives up his life to save the inhabitants of a nearby town from a flood.

Ronald's success in "The White Sister" determined Mr. King to keep him on for another picture to be made in Italy. This was "Romola," in which Ronald once again supported Lillian Gish. The film did not achieve the popularity of its predecessor, being more scenic than dramatic; also Ronald's rôle was an ungrateful affair. It was not to harm his future, however, for he had attracted the attention of Samuel Goldwyn, one of the heads of United Artists, who engaged him to play a leading part in George Fitzmaurice's production of "Tarnish." Satisfied with Ronald's work, Mr. Goldwyn then offered him a long-term contract, which has proved so satisfactory that it is still in force.

Ronald Colman

Among his next pictures were "A Thief
in Paradise," "The Sporting Venus," "Her
Sister From Paris," in which Ronald
played with Constance Talmadge, and then,
the "Dark Angel," beginning his partnership with Vilma Banky. The film was romantic and tragic, and the two players, one
darkly handsome and the other golden-
haired and radiantly beautiful. Ronald
played the part of a British officer, called
away to war before he can marry the girl
he loves. Invalided back to England,
blind, he hides his affliction, and pretends
that he no longer cares for her. In the end
she discovers his deception and comes to
him in her wedding dress. The picture was
a romantic and sentimental success, setting
susceptible audiences weeping all over the
country. None the less, some months were
to elapse before the real Colman and

143

Banky partnership was to be made more or less permanent.

Following "The Dark Angel," Ronald made his appearance in "Stella Dallas," with Belle Bennett, Lois Moran, and Jean Hersholt. He then appeared in Ernst Lubitsch's production of Oscar Wilde's famous comedy, "Lady Windermere's Fan," a Warner Brothers picture. For his next film, "Kiki," he went to First National, to support Norma Talmadge who was playing the title rôle. To American audiences Ronald's most endearing picture is "Beau Geste," Herbert Brenon's famous production for Paramount, which was released in August of 1926. Ronald Colman, Ralph Forbes and Neil Hamilton, played three quixotically romantic English boys who run away from home to shield the reputation of a beloved aunt, enlist in the Foreign

144

Legion, and experience the most romantic and tragic adventures culminating with the death of "Beau" Geste, the moving spirit of the trio, in a besieged fort in the Arabian desert. Ronald was the most ideal choice for the part of "Beau": quizzical, gallant, courageous, and gaily romantic, he brought vividly to life the most successful characterization that ever came from the pen of Percival Christopher Wren.

"Beau Geste" proved something of a triumph for all concerned, and Ronald returned to United Artists in a blaze of glory. His next film was "The Winning of Barbara Worth," in which he was again co-starred with Vilma Banky. This was a story of the West, photographed in color, beautifully set, and well acted, of more interest, perhaps, for its backgrounds than for the story it told. The public seemed

145

to enjoy the Colman-Banky combination; the studio endeavored to provide them promptly with more pictures in which the two were together. "The Night of Love" was the next in order. Here the two played in a Spanish setting: wishing revenge, a romantic bandit, Ronald, kidnaps a beautiful princess, Miss Banky, on the eve of her marriage. The natural result, of course, is love at first sight, and the solution is worked out according to the most approved traditions of romance. "The Magic Flame," also very successful, told an entertaining and exciting story about two delightful young circus performers who become separated through circumstances having to do with mistaken identity.

With the release of "Two Lovers," in September, 1928, the successful partnership was brought to an end. Both stars had achieved such popularity together that it was thought better to separate them and develop them individually. "Two Lovers," a romance of the Netherlands during the Spanish occupation, was a spectacular conclusion as well as an entertaining film.

Ronald's first starring film was "The Rescue," taken from Joseph Conrad's novel of the same name. It was a highly interesting, very dramatic, and tragic story, proving that a man fails because of inward weakness, not from outward circumstances. Ronald was hardly the burly Tom Lingard of Conrad's creation, but he gave none the less a very fine, sympathetic, and plausible characterization. "The Rescue" was the last silent picture in which he was to appear; it was released in January of 1929.

In August of that same year came "Bulldog Drummond," and Ronald Colman, in one bound, established himself at the top of the list of actors who had made good in talking films. Being able to make use of his voice was a tremendous asset, for his quiet, cultivated, English speech, his gentlemanly manner, and his charming *savoir faire* were as welcome, in those desperate days of raucous sounds, as an oasis in the desert. "Bulldog Drummond" was the famous old detective story by "Sapper" and proved fair game for Mr. Colman and the studio in the pleasing task of satirizing melodrama. Mr. Colman enjoyed himself immensely, as did the other actors; while audiences, expecting to shiver, reveled in Ronald's nonchalant acceptance of the most hair-raising situations. It was in this film that Joan Bennett made her screen debut, charmingly portraying the rôle of the bewildered and persecuted heroine.

148

For Ronald's second talking picture, a
somewhat different subject was selected:
Blair Niles' grim narrative, "Condemned
to Devil's Island." Ronald played the part
of a French convict sentenced to the dread-
ful penal colony in the same cheerful fashion in which he had previously romped
through "Bulldog Drummond." The film
was entertaining and possessed many beautiful backgrounds. Ann Harding had the
leading feminine rôle of the beautiful and
unhappy young wife of the bestial com-
mandant; her love scenes with Mr. Colman
were exquisitely played. With "Raffles,"
Ronald Colman came back to the drawing
room once more and re-entered the atmosphere in which he seems most at home. The
film was somewhat loosely derived from the
celebrated "Raffles" stories by Hornung,
showing in entertaining fashion the efforts

of the amateur cracksman to give up his criminal ways and lead a free life in the best of London society. Acted throughout with a light touch, the film depended for its effect upon Mr. Colman's deftness and humor, an assignment which he lived up to without difficulty.

The United Artists recently engaged Frederick Lonsdale, the British playwright, to write an original story which developed into "The Devil to Pay," a gay comedy of the black sheep of a conservative English family, who turns up most inopportunely from Africa, buys a dog with the last of his money, and sets his relatives very neatly by the ears. Mr. Colman and the delightful wire-haired fox-terrier made such a hit that he purchased the dog when the picture was completed and retired him from the screen. "The Devil to Pay" was succeeded by "The Unholy Garden," a tale of adventure and romance in foreign parts. It was written for Mr. Colman's use by Ben Hecht and Charles McArthur, authors of "The Front Page."

Ronald Colman has now attained a position so comfortable that he would not be likely to desire to change positions with anyone in his profession. His particular brand of ironic humor, his gift for playing romantic, even serious drama, his pleasant voice and engaging manner bring to his films the stamp of gentlemanliness and easy good breeding that endears him to so many of the more fastidious lovers of the screen. By his own admission, he prefers comedy and will, if possible, confine himself to this type of picture. Despite this, he has undertaken to play the title rôle in a screen version of Sinclair Lewis' novel, "Arrowsmith," which marks a distinct departure from his usual sort of parts, inasmuch as he will undertake to portray a young American doctor.

He takes very calmly all the adulation he receives and goes serenely on his way, keeping out of the public eye as much as is feasible. Whether he remains in talking pictures indefinitely is a question that he himself is not as yet prepared to answer. His own testimony would indicate that he might return to the stage once more, an event which has been prophecied many times but which his continued popularity in films has always prevented. The screen's foremost romantic actor, and the only one we know of who can be whimsical without causing active discomfort, he leads the life of a reserved English gentleman, indulging on occasion in his favorite sports, tennis and cricket. The public is intensely interested in him, all the more for his retiring qualities and a very natural reticence about his personal affairs. Attractive, intelligent, aloof and charming, he brings to his work an indefinable quality of glamor that sets him apart from his fellows.

GARY COOPER

GARY COOPER'S hold upon the romantic imagination of screen audiences in this country, and indeed, wherever English is understood, has grown with every film in which he has appeared. Just what makes him so fascinating a personality is not quite easy to discover, for even his most enthusiastic admirers will admit that he is neither a really great actor nor versatile to a great degree. Truth to tell, he is not really handsome either. But his personal charm is great. His slightly awkward angularity, the suggestion of boyish embarrassment in moments of sentiment; above all, the singularly appealing smile which lights up his normally rather solemn countenance,

154

and his pleasant, drawling speech—all these win the approval of a public that prefers its heroes strong, fairly silent and romantically tall, with a suggestion of mystery and world weariness thrown in.

If it were not for "Morocco," one might be tempted to set him down as a one-type actor, but the facility which he displayed in this fascinating combination of satire and sentiment, for cynical humor, lightness of touch, and genuine power of characterization, leads to the belief that there is far more to his ability than has been disclosed thus far in his films.

Gary Cooper did not set out to be a motion picture actor: in fact it was only after he found it impossible to make headway in his chosen profession, art, that he turned to films as an alternative. He was born in Helena, Montana, on May 7, 1902, his parents being Charles H. and Alice H. Cooper, both of whom are still living. For nine years he lived in Helena, after which his parents took him to England. During the three and one half years spent in that country, he attended grammar school at Dunstable, Bedfordshire. When he was thirteen years of age, his father and mother returned to Helena, and Gary then entered high school. The normal course of his life was suddenly interrupted shortly thereafter when he was so badly injured in an automobile accident that it became necessary for him to leave school entirely and go to his father's ranch in another part of the state in order to recover his health. The training and experience that he gained there, living an outdoor life and riding the range were to prove invaluable to him later. For two years he lived the life of a cowboy,

156

and in that way recovered his health and laid the foundation for his rugged physique and capacity for enduring all kinds of hardships.

By 1918 he was well enough to give up this out-of-doors existence and accordingly set out to complete his education. He entered Iowa College at Grinnell, Iowa, but the desire for a college education could not hold Gary indefinitely, and after two years he decided to return home and take up something in which he was really interested. For the next four years he worked as a cartoonist on one of the Helena newspapers before venturing to carry his talents to a wider market. On Thanksgiving Day, 1924, he came to Los Angeles with his sketch-book under his arm and the determination in his mind to become a commercial artist. Business men do not always recognize budding talent, however, and at one of the several advertising firms where Gary applied for work, he was offered the opportunity, not to paint or to draw, but to sell display space. He accepted it, but did not like the work, although for three months he struggled along and tried to make a success of it. It was no use: the work was uncongenial to him, and there was something more exciting in view, provided he could qualify.

Accordingly, in March, 1925, Gary Cooper made his first venture into motion pictures as an extra. His stature and his ability to ride almost any sort of a horse brought him a considerable number of small assignments providing atmosphere in big outdoor pictures. For the space of a year he kept at it and then was given his first chance at a real part. Hans Tiesler, an independent producer on the famous and now extinct "Poverty Row," asked Gary to play in a two-reeler. Eileen Sedgwick was his first leading lady. The release of this short picture called attention to Gary's possibilities and gradually he found small parts coming his way with greater and greater frequency. His real chance came when he was offered the rôle of Abe Lee in "The Winning of Barbara Worth," an all-color United Artists production in which Ronald Colman and Vilma Banky were co-starred. At that time Gary was not under contract to any studio in particular, but his work in "The Winning of Barbara Worth" brought him to the favorable attention of B. P. Schulberg, general manager of West Coast Production for Paramount.

Without telling him what was in the wind, Mr. Schulberg summoned Gary to his office, and when the latter stepped into the doorway, he found himself confronted by an assemblage consisting of all the departmental executives in the studio. Not knowing what else to do, Gary smiled that now famous smile—Mr. Schulberg smiled back and told him to wait outside. One can imagine Gary pacing the corridor for half an hour, wondering what was going to happen, then Mr. Schulberg called him back to offer him a contract. The opinion of all present had been so unanimously favorable that Gary was not even asked to take a test, and the episode of his engagement ranks as the first successful camera-less test on record.

Paramount lost no time in putting their new acquisition to work and Gary was soon playing the part of a newspaper reporter in "It," Clara Bow's first starring medium.

160

His work was considered so satisfactory in
this film that immediately he was cast as
Ted Larabee, the happy-go-lucky hero of
"Children of Divorce," in which Clara
Bow and Esther Ralston were co-starred.
Perhaps the first rôle in which he made an
outstanding impression on the public was
that of Cadet White in the celebrated
"Wings," the most famous of the early avia-
tion dramas. In the two central rôles were
Richard Arlen and Charles Rogers, but
Gary was decidedly interesting as the attractive, reticent youth whose plane crashed
about half way through the film. His performance here paved the way for several
films of war in the air in which he was
later to appear. For the time being, however, Paramount decided to try him out in
Western dramas, an idea which proved hap-
pier than their wildest dreams. The first

two stories of this sort in which Gary rode horseback and swung a lariat were "Arizona Bound," and "Nevada." The latter was the story of a gunman who saves the herds of the girl he loves and exposes one of the trusted ranch hands as a thief. In the supporting cast one finds the name of William Powell, who was to appear prominently in the next of Gary's starring films.

This picture was "Beau Sabreur," a badly mutilated and rather silly screen version of the second in the popular series of Foreign Legion novels by Percival Christopher Wren. Gary played the part of a French officer in a somewhat unconvincing manner, and Mr. Powell, as usual in those days, that of a particularly dastardly spy. This film was released in January, 1928. Then came "The Legion of the Condemned," a romantic drama of daredevil aviators who

Gary Cooper

have enlisted in the service with the sole purpose of being killed. The hero, played by Mr. Cooper, believes his sweetheart faithless when he finds her in the arms of a German officer, but later discovers that her actions were prompted by patriotic reasons, as she is a spy. "Doomsday," the next in order, was something of a contrast, being the story of a girl who marries her rich suitor, decides she has made a mistake, and is then allowed to enter a six-months probation course on the ranch of her impecunious lover, after which she marries him. It was a highly moral picture, forcefully emphasizing the inability of money to buy happiness.

Following "Doomsday," Gary went to First National Pictures to play with Colleen Moore in "Lilac Time." The title and the name of the heroine were taken from

163

a play by Jane Cowl, but the plot was entirely rewritten and became the drama of a little French girl and a handsome American aviator, billeted in her house with his friends, all of whom have an alarming fondness for death. Everything ends happily with a reunion in a big hospital in Paris. This was a serious and tearful representation, in startling contrast with Gary's next film, "Half a Bride." In this he played the part of the captain of a yacht owned by a wealthy man who has his spoiled daughter kidnapped and placed aboard. While shipwrecked, the captain and the girl fall in love, and when they are rescued, she decides to marry for good, not—as she had once planned—for six months. Another pleasing but unimportant film made by Gary that season was "The First Kiss," in which he took the part of a shabby South-

164

ern boy who falls in love with an aristocratic girl and then turns river pirate to educate his three brothers.

The most notable film of the year 1928 in which Gary played a leading rôle proved to be "The Shopworn Angel." It was one of the last silent films produced by Paramount and one of the best. It tells a simple, poignant story of an unsophisticated soldier from Texas who falls in love with an attractive chorus girl, mistress of a wealthy man-about-town; he gradually wins her love, her character changes completely, and they are married just before he sails to France. Gary Cooper's portrayal of the lovable, blundering, honest youth remains one of the best things he has ever done, while the splendid work of Nancy Carroll and Paul Lukas gave indication of their future stardom.

In the first months of 1929, Gary played in "Wolf Song," and "Betrayal." The former told about a restless young scout who finds himself constantly lured away from the girl he loves by the call of the wilderness. In this picture Gary appeared for the first time with the diminutive and fiery Lupe Velez. To this day, no one knows, except themselves, whether they are married yet or not, but there is no question about their being in love. "Betrayal" was the last film in which Emil Jannings was to appear in this country, and Gary was necessarily subordinated. Nevertheless, he gave an excellent performance of a young artist, in love with the wife of a Swiss bourgeois but unable to win her away from her husband. This was the last silent picture in which Gary was to play: the coming months brought the sound film.

Since Gary was then, as he is now, one of the most popular stars under contract to Paramount, every effort was expended to make his first talking picture a success. A happy chance brought about the selection of Owen Wister's famous novel, "The Virginian." Gary Cooper seemed predestined for the part of the quiet and dangerous young man whose retort to his enemy's insults was: "When you call me that, smile!" The production itself was superb and the authentic atmosphere of the old West was splendidly conveyed. One enjoyed Gary's work throughout for its general level of excellence: his unspoken affection for Steve, the luckless friend whom he was obliged to hang, was masterfully portrayed, and his love scenes with Molly Wood, the pretty school-teacher from the East, were played with delicacy and restraint. In cow-

167

boy costume he seemed thoroughly in his element, and the manner with which he handled his horse or merely strode through the woods was a pleasure to watch.

Equally admirable, although in an entirely different key, was "Seven Days' Leave," taken from Sir James Barrie's poignant little play, "The Old Lady Shows Her Medals." It was virtually a duet between Gary, as Kenneth, and Beryl Mercer, as Mrs. Dowey, the old lady who pretended that she had a son and then found that she did, after all. These two characters were simple people, not very expressive: one was timid, the other suspicious. Kenneth is a private in the famous Black Watch regiment; Mrs. Dowey is a charwoman who felt that she was of no use in war time, since she had no son. Accordingly, she writes letters to herself from an imaginary son

whom she calls Kenneth. When the real
Kenneth Dowey materializes, he is inclined
to be distrustful, but spends his leave with
the old lady who is at first overwhelmed
and then filled with wonderful joy, and ends
by asking her to be his mother. It is safe
to say that Gary will never surpass his performance of the dour, lean young Scotch-
man: at first puzzled and wary, and then
finally responding in kind to the adoration
of the old lady. One will not easily forget
the touching scene in which he asked her
to be his mother. It is regrettable that the
picture was too quiet to prove a popular
success, but it is something of which Gary,
Miss Mercer and Richard Wallace, (the
director), have every reason to be proud.

Gary's films were still steadily improv-
ing, and his next two, while not remarkable,
provided excellent entertainment. One

was "Only the Brave," a pretty little romance that started out to be a straight Civil War and spy drama and ended by being rather a clever satire on the flowery narratives of the period. "The Texan," next on the list, taken from an O'Henry short story, "A Double-Dyed Deceiver," proved to be an amusing, fairly exciting sketch, in which the author's neat little ironic twist was almost effaced by a serious and needlessly dramatic conclusion. Aside from taking part in "Paramount on Parade," Gary made his next appearance in "The Spoilers." This celebrated novel by Rex Beach had already been screened twice, but the talking version, ending with the ferocious fight between Mr. Cooper and William Boyd, left little to be desired. The narrative unwound somewhat slowly, but the setting was picturesque, faithfully depicting Alaska in the days of the Gold Rush, and Gary was seen to excellent advantage as the perplexed young prospector who is persuaded to leave the justice of his claims to the law at the risk of losing everything.

More recently Gary appeared in "Morocco," giving a performance that should rank with his work in "Seven Days' Leave," "The Shopworn Angel," and "The Virginian." Most notable was the fact that here his acting struck a new note, and struck it with the utmost conviction. Hitherto he had been playing serious, upright, rather inarticulate young men, but in "Morocco" he was given the rôle of a carefree, cynical soldier of fortune, to whom love affairs were matters of the most minor importance. He played the part splendidly and his performance is notable in a film of interest primarily because of its introduction of Marlene Dietrich to the American public. With this excellent achievement behind him, he acted a Western drama, "Fighting Caravans," by Zane Grey. This film was a distinct disappointment: the story was thin and too disjointed, and Gary's interest in the proceedings was at a very low ebb. "City Streets," another recent film, proved an abrupt contrast. It is a story of modern city life and Gary's part is that of a young man unwillingly drawn into a criminal career to save the girl he loves.

Whatever he does is sure to attract interest and enthusiasm. The only thing that can put a stop to his successful career is overwork: he is too popular for his own good and consequently he will be kept busy incessantly without rest or vacation. Over six feet in height and inclined to be slender, he needs to watch over his expenditure of energy and not be too prodigal of his strength. Fame carries its penalties, one of which is being obliged to produce more films than one man can handle. Gary Cooper, with his red-brown hair, blue eyes, and disarming smile, is not likely to outlive his popularity. He gives the public what it wants and should, accordingly, be given only good pictures and then not too many for him to do his best in each. He has proved his ability as an actor, but he has also earned the right not to be hurried or forced to waste his talents on inferior stories.

DOUGLAS FAIRBANKS

JUST as there is only one Charlie Chaplin, so there is only one Douglas Fairbanks,—and little chance that there will ever be another. Douglas Fairbanks fills a niche in the hearts of the American screen public—indeed, of the screen public all over the world—that he has made indisputably his own. His abounding good humor, emphasized by that infectious smile and those white even teeth; his amazing vitality, his good sportsmanship, and his unwillingness to be satisfied with anything less than the best—these are the characteristics that have endeared him to millions who will forget a legion of more skillful actors and actresses sooner than

"Doug." He is the small boys' hero, and as such appeals to the small boy in everyone. He is the very essence of vigorous, full-blooded romance—romance frank and unashamed, designed to please and to thrill, not to educate. Those spectacular productions of his—"The Mark of Zorro," "The Thief of Bagdad," "The Three Musketeers," "The Black Pirate," "Robin Hood," "The Iron Mask," "The Gaucho," and "Don Q"—are all artistically made, true to their periods, and above all, exciting, entertaining and robust. They were, moreover, clean from start to finish, and it is no small thing for any one man to turn out so many successful productions without ever introducing an offensive note.

Douglas Fairbanks' career has been crammed with action, excitement, and accomplishment, from the days when he first began leaping through the windows in those lively comedies which marked the start of his histrionic life in New York, to the present time when he makes a picture only if the spirit moves him, spending the rest of his time traveling and playing golf. The amount of work he has accomplished in the intervening twenty-five years is enough to stagger the imagination.

It has often been said that nothing is impossible to diligence and skill, and Douglas Fairbanks has been liberally endowed by nature with these valuable attributes. Nothing is too hazardous for him to try, nothing too difficult to be undertaken, if it is for the good of the picture. More than once, he has barely escaped being killed in the performance of dangerous stunts that he refused to allow doubles to handle. With him it has been all in the game, and a splendid game, too. If he carries out his threat, often repeated and never fulfilled, of retiring from pictures altogether, he will leave a record of which he may justly be proud, and for which the public has every reason to be grateful.

Douglas Fairbanks was born in Denver, Colorado, on May 23, 1884. His father was a lawyer from New York who had come to the West to examine some mining properties and decided to remain there. For the first two years of his life, he did little but cultivate an immense curiosity, keep his parents constantly on the jump, and develop his muscles for future use. Then, one fine day, at the age of two, he climbed out on the roof of a shed and made his first jump—ten feet to the ground. Even in those days he was apparently tough, but that leap left him with a scar on his forehead and the mark is visible today in spite of makeup.

Mr. Fairbanks senior was a great student of Shakespeare, and before his son was in his teens had read the great dramas to him. Douglas was so fascinated by the sound of the words that he began to memorize the famous speeches long before he had an inkling of what they meant. He loved to declaim for the benefit of his father's theatrical friends—it is said that at the age of ten he would recite "To be or not to be" with a vigor that made up for the lack of correct emphasis. By the time he was seventeen years old, his parents moved back to New York, and Douglas sought an opening in a theatrical company. With his head so full of Shakespeare, it was not long before he found a position with the company of the well-known classic actor, Frederick Warde, who was a friend of his father, and glad enough to give the fledgling actor a chance to try his wings. As usually happens in such cases, Doug was first given only bits to play, but by the time the company had traveled as far as Duluth he was promoted to playing Cassio and Laertes. He still remembers a newspaper notice that read: "Mr. Warde's supporting company was bad, but worst of all was Douglas Fairbanks as Laertes." While willing to admit, both then and now, that he was far from being an unqualified success, Douglas says that he tried hard, and for a while did not know what was the matter with his acting. Finally he came to the conclusion that it was lack of what is known as higher education. Accordingly, when Mr. Warde's season was at an end, he came to Harvard and enrolled as a special student, his credits from the Denver public schools and the

Colorado School of Mines not permitting him to enter as a full-fledged freshman. For five months he stuck to elementary Latin, French, and English literature, but that was enough. The theatre still lured him, so he went back to New York and there obtained an engagement with Effie Shannon and Herbert Kelcey in "Her Lord and Master."

Seized by the wanderlust when the run of the play was over, he shipped on a cattle-boat for Europe, with two young friends. Adventurous like himself each of them had fifty dollars in cash and they worked their way over, had a marvelous time, and were home again in three months.

This time Douglas decided that he would try something else than the stage, and so he went in for high finance in Wall Street. Starting as a salesman, he became, before

six months were up, head of the order department of the brokerage house of DeCop-
pet & Doremus. He says that he resigned
in a panic lest his superiors find out how
little he really knew about his job. Un-
daunted by this experience, he obtained a
position in a hardware factory, only to give
it up when he discovered how meager would
be the reimbursement for years of toil.

After all it was to be the stage, he decided, and returned to it without further
experimenting. For a year he acted in support of Alice Fisher in "Mrs. Jack." The
engagement came to an end after he had
had some very high words with the company manager who objected to his playing
every other rôle in the production as well
as his own.

Next on his list of occupations came the
law, a three months' effort which was dis-

rupted by a sudden and violent desire to go to Japan. He started, accordingly, but had traveled only as far as London when he encountered an old friend and forgot all about his desires to see the Orient.

Back he came to New York and resumed acting, this time under the management of William A. Brady. This association was to continue for seven years, off and on, and the two men, actor and manager, both filled to the brim with noise and energy, found it an excellent combination. "Doug" first forced himself on Mr. Brady's notice when he hurtled through a crowd of three hundred extras in "The Pit," and made himself both seen and heard. Complete accord between them was lacking after a while on account of the little matter of salary, so for a time "Doug" went elsewhere. He played first in a melodrama called "Two

Little Sailor Boys," and then in his only musical comedy, "Fantana," sponsored by the Shuberts. No doubt he enjoyed it, in part, although he never could get beyond the first few bars of the song.

Finally Mr. Brady came to the conclusion that there was no reason why a matter of money should stand between him and one of the most promising specimens of star material that he had ever seen. Accordingly he telegraphed "Doug," offering him a five-year contract which so astonished the recipient that he telegraphed back to Mr. Brady for a confirmation. Soon after this he saw his name in lights as the star of "Frenzied Finance." Unfortunately, this play was not a success, and while waiting for Mr. Brady to select another play, "Doug" supported Grace George (Mrs. Brady) in "Clothes," and later appeared in

183

leading comedy rôles in "The Man of the Hour" and "As Ye Sow." Mr. Brady then found another play for him, "All for a Girl," but this too failed after a short run. In desperation, Mr. Brady made a place for "Doug" in "The Gentleman From Mississippi," co-starring him with Tom Wise. This play ran for a year and proved of great value in establishing Doug as a capable player of light comedy rôles. There followed "The Cub" and "A Gentleman of Leisure," both reasonably successful. During the run of the latter play, "Doug" and Mr. Brady agreed to part company, and by ten o'clock the next morning "Doug" had signed a starring contract of five years duration with Cohan and Harris.

Wonderful as this seemed, there appeared to be some difficulty in finding a suitable play, even though Mr. Cohan promised to

184

write one especially suited to "Doug's" talents. Having nothing to do in the meantime, "Doug" went to Cuba, walked across the island, took a ship for Yucatan, walked from Progresso to Merida, and came back to find the play still unfinished. To kill more time, "Doug" went into vaudeville with a sketch called "A Regular Business Man," and shortly afterwards was sent to Chicago to play the leading part in "Officer 666." While he was out there, Lewis Waller suggested "Hawthorne, U. S. A.," one of his own plays, which had theretofore been presented only in London, as a good vehicle for "Doug." This experiment proved highly successful and for the first time "Doug" had the opportunity to be as athletic on the stage as he was off. He vaulted over walls, jumped from balconies, and ended with a marvelous free-for-all

185

fight. Following "Hawthorne, U. S. A.," came "He Comes Up Smiling," "The New Henrietta," and "The Show Shop,"—all successes.

It was during this season, which later proved to be his last on Broadway, that Douglas Fairbanks received an offer of two thousand dollars a week from D. W. Griffith to act in motion pictures. The proposition was too good to refuse, and in the summer of 1914, "Doug" made his first picture, "The Lamb." It was a hit from the first showing, and the new screen player was deluged with offers from other studios. Triangle Films, of which Mr. Griffith was then the head, offered him a three-year contract at two thousand dollars a week with a raise of five hundred dollars a week every six months. The offer was accepted and "Doug" settled down—

186

Douglas Fairbanks

speeded up, rather—to earning his living as a screen star. Because of his abundant and abounding energy he was given parts calling for such strenuous exertion that he was soon looked upon as an acrobat, rather than an actor. This was not altogether fair, for what he had really done was to speed up the tempo of screen playing. Camera men became groggy and directors dizzy, but his pictures assuredly moved, and moved fast. He was oblivious to what the older inhabitants of Hollywood thought or said; he knew what he was after, and D. W. Griffith found it wiser to allow him a free rein. For Triangle Films, "Doug" made "The Lamb," "Double Trouble," "His Picture in the Papers," "The Americano," "The Habit of Happiness," "The Matrimaniac," "Flirting With Fate," "The Good Bad Man," "The Half Breed," "Manhat-

187

tan Madness," and "American Aristocracy."

When it became apparent that Mr. Griffith would be unwilling to conform to the preliminary understanding by which he was to supervise all the Fairbanks productions, "Doug" went to Famous Players. For them he made "In Again, Out Again," "Wild and Wooly," "Down to Earth," "The Man from Painted Post," "Reaching for the Moon," (the silent picture) "A Modern Musketeer," "Headin' South," "Mr. Fix-It," "Say, Young Fellow," "Bound in Morocco," "He Comes Up Smiling," the famous "Arizona," and "The Knickerbocker Buckaroo."

Once these were completed, he undertook to form his own production company and began work with "His Majesty the American," following it with "When the Clouds Roll By," "The Mollycoddle," and

"The Mark of Zorro," the last of which is held by many to be the best film he has ever produced.

This latter picture, made soon after he joined forces with Mary Pickford and Charles Chaplin in the formation of the organization to be known henceforth as "United Artists," was his first venture into straight romantic costume drama. It gave full play to his athletic inclination, too,— this time with sword-play rather than fisticuffs. Perhaps not altogether satisfied with his own efforts in the new type of film (although the public reception of "Zorro" might have reassured him), in his next production he reverted to farce comedy; it was called "The Nut."

With romantic fire now in his veins he went for his following picture to Alexandre Dumas, romanticist *par excellence,* and

chose "The Three Musketeers." The part
of D'Artagnan had always appealed to him
greatly, and his affection for the story resulted in a truly magnificent production.
Those whose knowledge of Dumas was possibly too keen for comfort, found that the
result favored Douglas more than Dumas,
but it was all great fun, nevertheless. If
"Doug" did not look like the fiery young
Gascon, at least he acted like him. What
more could anyone ask? The success of the
production—for its enormous popularity
more than repaid Mr. Fairbanks the good-
sized fortune he had put into its production
—determined him to follow it up with other
romantic costume dramas. The first of
these was "Robin Hood," a marvelously
beautiful production in the veritable spirit
of the Middle Ages. Settings, costumes and
acting were all keyed together in a vast and

realistic whole that recreated the period to a remarkable extent. In this picture "Doug" performed some of his most astonishing acrobatic feats, and for the first and only time used a double in a perilous episode—the occasion when Robin Hood rides up to the castle moat as the drawbridge starts to rise, climbs on to it and then runs up the massive chain to the sally port.

After "Robin Hood" came the "Thief of Bagdad," possibly the most beautiful and elaborate production that he ever made. It was a fantastic production of the Arabian Nights story, with the flying carpet, the flying horse, the rope running up into the sky, an immense army raised from nothing by magic powder—all the paraphernalia of fairy tales on a gigantic scale. The money that went into the production of that film was not recovered, for the public was unable to appreciate so extraordinary a fantasy. Nevertheless, it was a beautiful and entrancing piece of work, in which Mr. Fairbanks, as the half-naked rascal who sets out to win a princess, gave a joyous and exhuberant performance. It is to be hoped that he did not regret the pains that he took, for it was a memorable achievement, and one that is not likely to be forgotten by those who were fortunate enough to see it.

The next production was "Don Q, Son of Zorro," an energetic and lively sequel to "The Mark of Zorro," not quite so good as its predecessor but excellent entertainment. He followed this in 1926 by "The Black Pirate," one of the earliest of the all-color pictures, and one of the most satisfying. It was an extremely beautiful but very costly production. The artist must have kept an eye on Howard Pyle's pirate drawings and paintings, for remarkably fine effects were produced by the use of browns and greens, with an occasional vivid dash of orange or red, and the contrasting blues of sky and ocean. The story was wild, often cruel, and more often than not, wholly incredible. No one minded, however, for romance is not expected to be true to life. Mr. Fairbanks was everywhere, as the young nobleman turned pirate to avenge his father's death, and made great play with sword, pistol and dagger.

His production for the year 1927 was something of a disappointment. "The Gaucho," as it was called, dealt with a group of picturesque South American cattle thieves, but there was too little plot, and an excess of religious symbolism. All this was forgotten, however, when Mr. Fairbanks went back to the days of the "The

Three Musketeers" and chose one of Dumas' own sequels, "The Man in the Iron Mask" for his picture of 1929. The story was somewhat disjointed—it covered a period of twenty years,—but the beauty of the presentation made ample amends. As D'Artagnan grown older, wiser, and sadder, "Doug" performed some of the finest acting he has to his credit. The production seemed something of a gallant gesture filled as it was with heroic deeds and undying devotion, and had a sad and tragic ending. Furthermore, despite its noisy prologue and epilogue, it was the last silent picture that Mr. Fairbanks was to make. The era of talking pictures was at hand. Although he did not like the new type of pictures and felt that they were no place for him, he consented to make "The Taming of the Shrew" in company with his wife,

Mary Pickford. Shakespeare in the talking films was not an unmitigated success,
although Mr. Fairbanks made an exuber-
ant, gay and picturesque Petruchio, speaking his lines with admirable clarity and
understanding. With "The Taming of the
Shrew" behind him, "Doug" decided to
take a rest, and went to England to witness
some golf tournaments. On his return he
was persuaded to take a leading rôle in
"Reaching for the Moon." This achieved
considerable success and may or may not
inspire him to try some more like it. Of late,
however, his energies have been focussed
on the making of glorified travel films.

Douglas Fairbanks' first marriage, with
Beth Sully, did not prove a success, and
they separated soon after their only child,
Douglas Fairbanks, Jr., was born on December 9, 1909. His second matrimonial

venture, with Mary Pickford, whom he married on March 28, 1920, has been extremely happy and successful. They have a beautiful home, "Pickfair," in Beverly Hills, which is the first spot that visitors to the picture colony always ask to see. He is very proud of the growing abilities of his son, but claims no credit for his rise to success. Douglas Fairbanks has been acting a long time; he has made all the money he needs, and it is only natural that he should wish to retire while he is still young enough to enjoy life. A decision on his part to do so, however, would be regrettable, for there is no one—and probably never will be anyone—to take the place of the inimitable "Doug."

DOUGLAS FAIRBANKS, JR.

To BE related to a celebrity is not always an unmixed blessing: if you do not believe it, ask a few of the unfortunates who are always known as "So-and-so's brother" or "The son of ——, the famous actor." Not only does it mean that as an individual you cease to exist, so far as the public is concerned, but it also means that any success you may achieve will be credited to your kinship with the brilliant member of the family clan. Against this intangible but ever-present handicap Douglas Fairbanks, Jr., only son of the one and only Douglas Fairbanks and his first wife, Beth Sully, has been fighting all his life. The fact that he has won his battle for recognition as an

197

actor in his own right speaks volumes for his courage and persistence, as well as serving to prove that he is the possessor of no mean gifts.

Contrasting father and son is a revealing and exceedingly interesting procedure. Their racial resemblance is remarkable, and Douglas, Jr., has been enabled thereby to give some exceedingly clever impersonations of his famous parent, but when it comes to acting, they are as far apart as the poles. The elder Fairbanks has won his fame in plays and pictures demanding exhuberant vitality, tremendous energy, and picturesque, imaginative detail. Every motion reveals his abounding enjoyment of life and an inexhaustible fund of healthy animal spirits. With his son, everything is different. Douglas, Jr., is quiet, rather gentle, not essentially humorous, but possessed of a capacity for genuinely intense emotion. He plays in modern dramas that give him the chance to project deep feeling, tragedy even, with a burning sincerity that is more than surprising for one of his comparatively tender years. Perhaps it is because he has seen so much and been through so many trying experiences that he is able to act as he does.

Douglas Fairbanks, Jr., was born in New York City on December 9, 1909. As his parents were divorced while he was still very young, he spent much of his youth in boarding school. He did not enjoy it and was frank to say so. One of his real consolations during this trying time was the development of his striking artistic ability. When only nine years old he painted a caricature of Raymond Hitchcock which the latter used on his billboards for years.

Meanwhile his mother had remarried and was able to take him abroad for study. They remained in Paris for a year and then returned to Pasadena where Douglas was once more enrolled in a private school. He found the routine of the life unbearable, and he begged his mother to take him abroad once more. A serious financial loss, which swept away all the money settled by Douglas Fairbanks upon his wife at the time of the divorce, had reduced her income to very little indeed. Since, however, it was possible to live comfortably in Paris for about half of what it would cost in this country, she and her son crossed the Atlantic once more and went to live in the Latin Quarter of Paris.

Pressed as they were for money, as they were too proud to ask for charity, Douglas and his mother knew what it was to be hungry, and more than once, too. These hard times came to an end when Paramount, realizing that Douglas Fairbanks' son was now sixteen years old, offered the boy a contract calling for four weeks' work at two thousand dollars a week. The picture produced was called "Stephen Steps Out"; it proved to be a failure. This was a great blow to the boy's pride, the more so when he discovered that he had been engaged solely on the strength of his father's reputation. So strongly was he opposed to trading on another man's reputation, even though that man be his own father, that he broke his contract, which called for another picture on the same terms. He was through with films until he could make a name for himself, unaided and strictly on his own merits. This was not so easy as it sounded, as he had no other source of income.

There was good stuff in the boy, however, for he set to work to make his art pay and in addition, began acting on the legitimate stage. Stubbornly refusing to be known merely as the son of Douglas Fairbanks, he took only such parts as he felt were offered to him because of his own merits. He rose gradually to more and more important rôles, playing in Los Angeles in "Romeo and Juliet," "The Jest," "Saturday's Children," "Toward the Light," Rupert Hughes' one-act drama, "The Ambush," and finally "Young Woodley." It was this last play that really paved the way for his return to films as an outstanding young actor. It is a very poignant and touching drama: the story of an English boy who falls idealistically in love with the beautiful wife of his head-master. For the Los Angeles opening, Douglas Fairbanks assembled his friends and went with a large party to give his son's picture a good reception. Those who went in a condescending mood, to applaud politely the son of a famous actor, remained to applaud that son on account of his undoubted excellence in a difficult part.

With this success behind him, Douglas Fairbanks, Jr., went back to motion pictures, taking with him the realization that he had made a definite start toward recognition as the possessor of an individual talent. He signed a new contract with Paramount and appeared first in support of Belle Bennett and Lois Moran in "Stella Dallas." It was a minor part, yet he made a definitely favorable impression. This film was made in 1925, and by the following season he had several pictures to his credit, among them "Padlocked," "Broken Hearts

of Hollywood," and "Manbait." Besides
acting, he found working with his father
on the technical end of the "Black Pirate"
a most interesting job. Taking cognizance
of his son's marked artistic and literary abilities, Douglas Fairbanks engaged him to
write the subtitles for the film and also to
design the costumes. Anyone who saw that
beautiful picture will agree that the picturesque garb of the pirates added enormously to the pleasing effect. Here also,
Douglas, Jr. found the Technicolor proc-
esses (the film was entirely in color) a
fascinating study, and since then he has
followed it up so assiduously that he has
become a recognized authority on this subject.

The following year, 1927, saw him con-
tinuing with his work behind the camera
as well as in front of it. He wrote the titles

for his father's next production, "The Gaucho," and also for "Two Lovers," the last film co-starring Ronald Colman and Vilma Banky. Films in which he appeared that season were "Women Love Diamonds," "Iz Zat So," and "The Texas Steer." Apparently the studio thought it best to keep him in comedies for a while, but he was making progress steadily, none the less. The year was particularly memorable for him in that he met and became engaged to Joan Crawford. This engagement was notable, not only for the fact that it lasted two years, owing to the youth of the participants, but also for the fact that it was so happy. Douglas and Joan went everywhere together and made no effort to conceal the fact that they were completely, unashamedly in love.

In 1928, he confined himself to acting

and writing for his own pleasure. Among the pictures that he made were "Our Modern Maidens," "Dead Man's Curve," "The Toilers," "The Power of the Press," and "The Barker." "Our Modern Maidens," one of a series of stories about modern youth, found him acting with Joan Crawford for the first and only time. It also gave him the opportunity to give impersonations of various screen celebrities, including his father. The picture was drama rather than comedy and allowed him to utilize his dramatic talent, which was developing so rapidly. Of the other films of the year in which he took part, the most notable was "The Barker," a sordid, powerful drama of circus life. The film proved highly successful, and his work was excellent.

When his Paramount contract came to

an end, Douglas decided to be a free lance for a while and during the year 1929 he appeared in many films, playing rôles of ever-increasing importance.

Perhaps the most striking bit of work he offered was in "A Woman of Affairs," with Greta Garbo. In this film—a thinly disguised version of Michael Arlen's "The Green Hat,"—he played the neurotic, over-sensitive brother of the heroine, an inflammable youth who always suspected the worst of everyone and died at a very early age. In the hands of most players it would have become unrelieved melodrama, tiresome and rather ridiculous, but somehow he put such sincerity into it, such over-wrought passion, that for the moment you actually believed the character to have existed. His other films of that year were "The Jazz Age," "Fast Life," "The Forward Pass," "Dance Hall," and "The Careless Age." These films portrayed the supposed affairs of the very young, forever drinking and dancing; the agonies of a youth condemned to death for a murder he did not commit; a mild football yarn; the pangs of adolescent love, and cruel disillusionment over a first love affair. "The Careless Age" tells how a sensitive boy, in love with a popular actress, tries to kill her when she throws him over for a wealthy admirer.

On June 3, 1929, Douglas Fairbanks, Jr., and Joan Crawford went to New York and were married at St. Malachi's Roman Catholic Church, having made the trip all the way from California in órder that the groom's mother might be present at the ceremony. They had no honeymoon, but returned at once to California to continue their work in pictures.

Douglas Fairbanks, Jr.

At this time Douglas began to publish his poetry and to contribute to "Vanity Fair" some extremely clever caricatures of motion picture stars, accompanied by brief character sketches. The drawings showed a very neat flair for satire, while the sketches, simply and clearly written as they were, displayed considerable literary aptitude. They indicated undisputably the presence of a talent capable of future development but by no means fully mature. Marriage proved something of a settling influence, however, and Douglas ceased to exhibit the impatience which he did in the past when he could not make his paint brush or his pencil do what he expected of them at the first try.

With the coming of the new year his parts became more notable than ever before, being rôles which, by dint of his fine playing, were to lead him to 'stardom. The year opened, not too auspiciously with "Loose Ankles," and "Party Girl," neither of which was sufficiently masterful as to cause much comment; but the best was soon to come. It came in the form of "The Dawn Patrol," a Richard Barthelmess picture in which Douglas had a part equal in importance to that of the star. The film was a war story, a tragedy of inexperienced young aviators sent out to die when they were hardly more than through school. There were no women in the story and little plot save the friendship of two young officers, separated by an unavoidable disaster, and finally reunited just before one takes the other's place on a mission that means sure death. All the acting was excellent, but that of Douglas Fairbanks, Jr., stood out above the rest. First National Pictures, the sponsor of the film and the company to which Douglas was under contract, decided to make him a star as a result of his performance.

Unfortunately, the will to create a star does not always insure that the right sort of pictures will be forthcoming to make the sudden giddy ascent secure. Douglas was loaned to Universal to take the leading rôle in "The Little Accident," and, while he did the best he could to struggle through a comedy part, he was out of his element. His acting was too forthright, too earnest, for flimsy situations that repeated themselves endlessly after the first few reels. Then came "One Night at Susie's," and "Outward Bound," both pictures being produced at the First National Studios. The former was a routine affair in which Douglas put his emotional sincerity to work on rather barren material. "Outward Bound," Vane Sutton-Vane's extraordinarily moving drama concerning the fate of the passengers on a mysterious ship that carries them from death to final judgment, found Douglas one of a notable cast. He played the part of a young man, who, with the girl he loved, had committed suicide in order that they might never be parted again. Arriving in the other world, they find that they are considered "Half-Ways," those who have killed themselves before their time, and as such are condemned to journey back and forth on the ghostly ship until they reach the hour appointed for their death on earth. All the players were so good that individual performances scarcely had a chance to stand out.

"The Way of All Men," taken from Henning Berger's "The Deluge," was

Douglas' next picture, but this also turned out to be something less than a triumph for the star. His part was less important than several others in the story, and his acting was not up to his usual high standard. The unfavorable impression left by this picture was quickly forgotten in the well deserved praise lavished upon "Little Caesar." This remarkable film of the underworld, splendidly directed and flawlessly acted, found Douglas co-starred with Edward G. Robinson, who played the title rôle. Owing to the picturesqueness of his rôle, Mr. Robinson took the foremost honors, but Douglas did fine, understanding work as the master criminal's one friend, who tried to go straight and was nearly killed for his attempt to do so. The entire production had a tremendous bite to it: the acid of truth for once was able to eat away the sentimen-

talism surrounding the motion picture portrayals of crime and gave the public a
glimpse of the realities of criminal life.

Next came Douglas' first real starring
film, bought for his use and produced with
his individual requirements in mind: this
was "Chances," a novel by A. Hamilton
Gibbs. It is the story of two brothers whose
devotion to one another is temporarily
ended when both find themselves in love
with the same girl. Following "Chances"
will come "I Like Your Nerve," a gay romantic comedy written especially by
Roland Pertwee for the use of young Mr.
Fairbanks.

For some time Douglas has said that
his greatest ambition is to appear in a screen
production of "L'Aiglon." The Edmond
Rostand play about the pitiful son of the
great Napoleon, is a beloved classic of the

French stage, and it is by no means improbable that it would prove effective on the screen. The boy, delicate of body, hedged about by the restrictions of the Austrian court at which no allusion to his famous father was ever permitted, cherished the fiery spirit and lofty aspirations of the little Corsican lieutenant who rose to rule the world. Too weak to withstand the opposition or to subdue the vaulting ambitions of his spirit, he died when only twenty-one. In France it is traditional for the rôle to be played by a woman, having been written for the use of Sarah Bernhardt, but no such tradition is in force here. One cannot think of any player better suited to act the part than Douglas Fairbanks, Jr.

One cannot help but feel that the studio to which Douglas Fairbanks is under con-

tract has a real responsibility, other, perhaps, than that of making money. He is
still very young, and yet he has behind him
the accomplishments for a far older man.
That he has unusually fine talent, no one
will deny. While by no means handsome,
he has so mobile a face and such expressive
eyes that the observer considers only what
he is feeling, not how he looks. In much
of his playing there is the impression of
strain—whether this is because he works
under high tension or merely because he
feels the character in question requires it,
cannot be said. Such youthful fire, if wisely
handled, can accomplish almost anything;
badly handled it may burn out too soon.

Above all, it should not be wasted on inferior films. It is to be hoped that he will
be wise enough to refuse shoddy material
and reserve his efforts for the best that can

be had. From the time of his first appearance on the screen, Douglas Fairbanks, Jr., has manifested great promise: now that that promise is on the brink of fulfillment, the utmost pains should be taken to insure that it will be developed with as little waste as possible.

He stands exactly six feet in height and is fond of various sorts of athletics. His father is his favorite golf opponent, though he beats him but very seldom. He also indulges in boxing, wrestling, swimming, and, in the past, was very good at track work. Although one would never guess it from his past career, he is quite frank in saying that he hates to work, but when he has to do it, no one works harder. For reading, he prefers serious subjects like biography, history and metaphysical philosophy, with a distinct bias in favor of literature having to do with the First Empire and with Napoleon. For his hobbies, there is music; and although he cannot tolerate grand opera, he goes to all the concerts he can find time to hear. In other words, he is accomplished, ambitious almost in spite of himself, and has a future that will repay any amount of watching.

WALTER HUSTON

IT IS more than possible that Walter Huston will go down in theatrical and motion picture history as the one actor who played Lincoln and was not handicapped thereby forever after.

There is something about impersonating the great Civil War President that sets an actor off in a class by himself where he finds himself so closely associated with the part that managers believe him incapable of doing anything else. It is a fate that has overtaken the best interpreters of Lincoln in the theatre and on the silent screen, and it is only by something closely approaching a miracle that Walter Huston has escaped. Perhaps it is the variety of rôles which he had played before undertaking the celebrated and perilous part in films; perhaps it is the fact that he did not sink himself altogether in the part and so proved that he was not out to be Lincoln for the rest of his natural life.

More than that, he had made so strong an impression in the theatre, playing Ephraim Cabot in Eugene O'Neill's "Desire Under the Elms" and the leading rôle in Kenyon Nicholson's "The Barker," that the reputation gained in these plays was enough to balance Lincoln and to prove that he was very far from being a one-part actor. As things stand now, he is one of the most interesting, stimulating, and completely satisfactory players in motion pictures. The reputation that he has made for himself is based on a composite of the various pictures and plays in which he has appeared,

not just on one strikingly truthful impersonation.

Walter Huston was born in Toronto,
Canada, in the year 1884, and spent his boyhood on a Canadian farm. His education
was pursued in a regulation fashion at the
Winchester Street school in Toronto, and
he did not even consider the stage as a
means of livelihood until 1902. The aspiring actor made his debut in a repertory
company playing in his native city, but,
desiring larger worlds to conquer, he took
a part with a traveling road show, which
promptly failed, leaving him to make his
way to New York by freight train. In view
of the rather serious type of stories in which
he has been acting of late, it is interesting
to remember that at this time Walter Huston was an expert on every sort of dancing
from ballroom steps to fast clogging, and

221

possessed an excellent singing voice. He was, however, totally unknown to the producers, who could hardly be expected to recognize in him a future dramatic star, and therefore found work hard to procure. At last he secured a position in a stock company playing a melodrama called "In Convict Stripes." This play was written by Hal Reid, Wallace Reid's father. Walter was given the central rôle and found himself playing with Lillian Gish, who had come to replace Mary Pickford. The production was a considerable success and Walter Huston soon found himself playing it on the road along with a very popular religious drama of the period, "The Sign of the Cross."

In those days actors were considered in somewhat the same light as thieves and vagabonds. Mr. Huston can recall the days

when Southern hotels posted the following
notice: "No dogs and actors allowed." He
also recalls a famous and disastrous occasion when, acting with Richard Mansfield,
he carried a spear for the honor of
Shakespeare and had four lines to speak,
but was so terrified that he forgot the four
lines and was forcibly ejected from the theatre by the irate Mr. Mansfield himself.
Notwithstanding this inauspicious start, he
played with Mansfield later on, but believes
that the temperamental star did not realize
that he was the same man. In the three
years between 1902 and 1905 he played continuously in stock and repertory and is of
the opinion that he played every possible
part known to the American stage save one
of the cakes of ice in "Uncle Tom's Cabin."

Apparently the stage did not seem very
promising, for in 1905 he abandoned it in

favor of business and went to work in city water and electrical plants in Nevada and Missouri. Winning a city engineer's license in St. Louis, he managed the Union Electric and Power Company's Charles Street plant. Four years of commercial life were enough, however, and in 1909 Walter Huston returned to the theatre.

This time, however, it was not stock company work that he undertook, but vaudeville, and he did not make the plunge alone. With him came his wife, Bayonne Whipple, and for the next fifteen years the team of Whipple and Huston played the Keith and Orpheum circuits, Huston contributing most of the acts himself. During those years he played practically every town of any importance in the United States and Canada.

About this time Brock Pemberton, fa-

224

mous New York producer, met Walter
Huston at a theatrical club and promptly
invited him to play the title rôle in "Mr.
Pitt," a play which Zona Gale had evolved
from one of her own stories. "Mr. Pitt"
opened at the 39th Street Theatre in New
York in January, 1924. The play itself was
a quiet, rather pathetic little story of a man
whose wife finds him too dull to live with
and whose son despises him, even after he
had made a fortune. There was nothing
heroic, nothing very dramatic, about the
story, but it was very appealing and extremely well acted. Walter Huston's characterization won him much praise, and the
rôle of the pathetic, futile Mr. Pitt, who
loved his wife and son desperately, yet
could win nothing but their half-contemptu-
ous tolerance, proved to be a stepping stone
to things of greater importance. It also

proved that those long years in stock and in vaudeville had been anything but wasted, for Walter Huston was one of the discoveries of the season.

His next part was that of Sam Crane in a brief engagement of "The Easy Mark."

With only two Broadway performances to his credit, Walter Huston was on the verge of attaining one of his most important parts. Eugene O'Neill, then struggling for the fame which was later to be his in such abounding measure, happened to see Mr. Huston on the stage and decided, then and there, that he was the very man to create the part of Ephraim Cabot in the first production of his grim drama of New England farm life, "Desire Under the Elms," which was about to be produced at the Greenwich Village Theatre. The première took place in November, 1924, and Walter Huston's stock took another sharp rise. Although only forty years of age, he gave so remarkable a portrayal of the stern old man of seventy-six that the playwright's choice was more than completely vindicated. The play itself was a powerful, sordid, and compelling work. Walter Huston caught and projected the mood with satisfying completeness. It is pleasant to know that in the first published edition of "Desire Under the Elms," Eugene O'Neill paid high tribute to Walter Huston and has recently affirmed his belief that Mr. Huston is one of the greatest of American actors.

The following year found Walter Huston again playing in a drama by Eugene O'Neill, one written in a very different mood. Constructed along the lines of ironic tragedy, it told the story of Ponce de Leon, the romantic Spanish explorer who spent his life in a vain endeavor to discover the mythical fountain of eternal youth. The play, appropriately entitled "The Fountain," did not achieve a long run, but Walter Huston's Juan Ponce de Leon was highly praised. The production took place at the Greenwich Village Theatre in December of 1925. While this is the only romantic costume drama in which Walter Huston has played, he experienced no apparent difficulty in turning from the harsh New England realism of "Desire Under the Elms" to the poetic fantasy of South America in the days when Spain was the most powerful country in the world.

Assuredly Mr. Huston can claim success in a series of the widely varied parts. From "The Fountain" he went to the grim melodrama of "Congo," which opened at the

228

Biltmore Theatre in March, 1926. This
play, later transferred to the silent screen
under the title of "West of Zanzibar," told
a grim story of the cruel revenge meted
out by a paralytic, living in the African
jungle, to the man who stole his wife. Mr.
Huston's performance was realistic and
filled with a sense of relentless cruelty and
sadistic, evil humor.

The following January came the second
of his great triumphs, "The Barker," by
Kenyon Nicholson, which opened at the
Biltmore Theatre and had a most successful
run of 221 performances. Mr. Huston's
part, later taken by Milton Sills in the
screen version of the play, was picturesque
and well supplied with dramatic dialogue
and strong situations. Mr. Huston played
it to the hilt, making so strong an impression upon his audiences that his name will

always be associated with this clever rôle.

From "The Barker," which mingled comedy and drama, Mr. Huston went to "Elmer the Great," a comedy, pure and simple. This delightful play, adapted by Ring Lardner from the short story, "Hurry Kane," and presented by George M. Cohan at the Lyceum Theatre, New York, on September 24, 1928, dealt with the adventures of Elmer Kane, who thought himself the world's greatest baseball player. Unfortunately the play did not attain the success that everyone expected and was discontinued after a run of only forty performances. There was no fault found with Mr. Huston, however, and he proved his right to be known as a clever comedian as well as a straight dramatic actor.

In the early spring of 1929, Walter Huston decided to try his fortune on the talking

Walter Huston

screen, and accordingly signed a contract with Paramount Pictures.

His first film was "Gentlemen of the Press," a former stage play, which dealt somewhat hysterically with the sad life led by newspaper men. His performance was satisfactory in every way, for he gave a consistent and believable portrayal of Wickland Snell, veteran reporter and news editor, who had an uncanny nose for news and an unhappy weakness for women. "Gentlemen of the Press" was quickly followed by "The Lady Lies," in which Claudette Colbert was co-starred with Mr. Huston. The picture was an excellent piece of work: splendidly acted and directed in the best of taste. This time Walter Huston played a middle-aged business man whose growing children disapprove violently of his relations with a charming young woman

231

outside the pale of matrimony. His acting and that of Miss Colbert were proof of the value of stage technique and well trained voices for the talking screen.

On the fourth of September, 1929, Walter Huston made another appearance in the theatre, playing the leading rôle in "The Commodore Marries," a play by Kate Parsons, which was produced by Arthur Hopkins at the Plymouth Theatre in New York. The author based her play on episodes from Smollett's famous novels, "Peregrine Pickle" and "Roderick Random," which described the rather pathetic effort of Commander Trunnion, retired from active duty with the British Navy, to lead a sea-going existence on shore, how his nautical régime was rudely broken in upon by his marriage with a designing woman, and how in the end he drives her out and settles back into

232

his former way of living. It was a *succes d'èstime* and failed to appeal to a sufficiently large public to make a long run possible. None the less, the notices received by Mr. Huston were such as might have tempted him to remain in the theatre. The reviewers, one and all, hailed his performance as a masterpiece of skillful characterization and the veritable incarnation of Smollett's blustering, honest, good-hearted, and shamelessly imposed upon character. When "The Commodore Marries" died a premature and much regretted death, Mr. Huston had finished with the stage for the time being.

Once more on the screen and still under the management of Paramount, he took the rôle of Trampas, one of the most celebrated bad men of literature or the drama, in the excellent screen version of Owen Wister's

233

"The Virginian," in which Gary Cooper played the title rôle. It was a portrait done with broad strokes, without much subtlety, but extremely effective; the aggressive moustache, the sinister voice, and the easy assurance of his playing made Trampas a memorable figure.

For Paramount he also appeared in a number of short films, among which were "The Bishop's Candlesticks"—an episode from Victor Hugo's "Les Miserables"— "The Carnival Man," and "Two Americans." In the last named he played the parts of General Grant and of Abraham Lincoln, a fact which may well have influenced D. W. Griffith in selecting him for the title rôle of his first talking picture, "Abraham Lincoln."

This film, which was to give Walter Huston the opportunity for the greatest acting he had yet contributed to the screen, presented something of a problem to actor and director alike. With so long and so full a life as Lincoln's to set before the public in less than two hours' time, it was necessary to omit a great deal. Mr. Huston had to develop his characterization as a series of somewhat disjointed episodes rather than as a connected story. In the completed picture his work was a remarkable and praiseworthy achievement. Although much like Lincoln in build, he did not resemble him facially until the period when historical accuracy called upon him to wear the famous beard; yet he went below the surface to an amazing degree and gave a very fine, rather poetic interpretation of Lincoln. One felt perhaps a certain lack of fire, and, at the same time an earthliness, in the portrayal. This impression was strengthened

235

by the fact that emphasis was placed on Lincoln's love for Ann Rutledge rather than on his statesmanship and greatness of soul. On the whole, however, it was a splendid characterization of which Mr. Huston had every reason to be proud.

With the completion of "Abraham Lincoln," Walter Huston returned to Paramount to make "The Virtuous Sin," adapted from a play entitled "The General," by Lajos Zillahy, and then went to First National for the filming of "The Bad Man." "The Virtuous Sin" was a very melodramatic and improbable play, which not even Mr. Huston's force and sincerity could make plausible. In "The Bad Man," taken from Porter Emerson Brown's stage play made memorable by Holbrook Blinn, he played a voluble Mexican bandit with a great display of flashing teeth and much misuse of the English language. His work was good, but all his makeup and picturesque costume could not conceal the fact that he was ill at ease in this quasi-romantic, quasi-satirical part.

"The Criminal Code," another former stage play, gave Walter Huston one of the finest opportunities yet vouchsafed him by the talking films. It was a grim, rather controversial drama of prison life as seen by a warden and by a boy whom he had sent to jail for an accidental killing. Mr. Huston played the part of a shrewd, business-like attorney who later becomes warden at a large penitentiary and there encountering the boy, now broken, disheartened, and sullen, is brought to a realization of what prison can do to a sensitive nature. There is no need to go into detail here: it is sufficient to say that Walter Huston built up his rôle skillfully and honestly, that he made his warden completely understandable alike in his harshness, his dawning regret, and his deep affection for his daughter.

Walter Huston has been married three times. He separated from his second wife, Bayonne Whipple, five years ago, and early last November they obtained a divorce. A few days after the decree became final, Mr. Huston married Ninetta Eugenia Sunderland, formerly his leading lady on the stage. By his first marriage he had one son, John, who is now working in Hollywood as scenario writer and sometimes as actor.

Mr. Huston's future is just about what he chooses to make it. He has proved his ability in all manner of rôles requiring forceful, sympathetic, and dramatic characterization. He can play comedy and trag-

238

edy; he can even play sentimental scenes
and be convincing. Among his gifts are
an excellent voice—powerful and expressive of varying emotions—and a face that,
for all its lack of regular features, has
proven singularly adaptable. His tall,
rangy, sinewy figure gives him the advantage of physicial dominance, a quality enhanced by his forthright personality. It is
by no means impossible that he may at some
future and not too distant date return for
a time to the stage—(he has voiced the desire to do so more than once)—but at present the films are making the most of his
unusual abilities. Whether on stage or
screen he is a consistently satisfying player
who can at all times be depended upon for
a superior performance.

EMIL JANNINGS

IF ONE had nothing else to do, it might be illuminating to take a few days off and count the number of times that the adjective, "great," is misapplied. Particularly amusing would it be in regard to motion pictures and motion picture players. Not a day goes by but that some mediocre film is hailed as "supremely great," or some fair to middling player as "the greatest actor of our generation." Truly the screen has taught us that the best way to render superlatives of no account is to use them all the time. In the theatrical world, there is less need to shriek so loudly for public attention, and words are used with more sense of their proper meaning, yet even there, numbers of "great" authors and "great" actors are discovered over night and disappear unnoticed. Perhaps "great" does not mean anything now, but to our way of thinking, there are a select few to whom it should be applied and to them alone. In the motion picture world, there are two actors who stand out so indisputably above their associates that there is but little argument over their rightful rank. One of these is Charlie Chaplin, supreme comic genius, the other, Emil Jannings, interpreter extraordinary of somber tragedy.

Sure proof of the quality of the art of these two men is the fact that they are known and admired all over the world. Both are supremely well qualified to express themselves in pantomime, needing no explanatory subtitles and no dialogue. The English language has proved a barrier to

Emil Jannings since the coming of talking films, but it will take more than that to disestablish his unequaled reputation. Say what you like about his acting—that it is too dreary, that he always dwells upon the disintegration of a man, or that he plays continually in the same sordid depressing vein—you cannot deny that the power, the emotional force, and the tremendous conviction, which he puts into every rôle, produce an effect which cannot be equaled by any other player of our day. His whole style of acting may be opposed to the restraint and casualness of most popular English and American actors, but by the very excess of his emotion, the mental and physical agony which he forces upon the spectator and drives home with merciless realism, we find the pity and terror that Aristotle declared to be the essentials of

242

true tragedy. It is not always pleasant nor invariably inspiring, but it is truth, and it is life.

So thoroughly German is Emil Jannings in appearance, in voice and in style of acting, that it may come as a surprise to many to learn that he was born in Brooklyn, New York, on July 29, 1886. The fact that his parents went back to Europe before Emil was a year old, is enough to explain his complete lack of Americanization. To be sure, his father and mother were both born in this country, and that fact was enough to save him from active military service during the late war, but while the German authorities considered him more or less an American, he himself has always felt that he was a German citizen. His father built up a moderate sized business manufacturing kitchen utensils in Brooklyn, but when the doctors ordered Mrs. Jannings to Switzerland for her health, he sold his business at a moderate profit and moved his entire family to Zurich. After a short time in the famous Swiss city, the Jannings menage made another move, this time to Görlitz, Germany, and there Emil received his first schooling.

For such a large and placid person as he appears to be off the screen, Emil Jannings led a very tempestuous boyhood. By the time he was fourteen years of age and had reached the fourth form in school, he decided that he did not desire any more education and ran away. His parents, wise enough not to force him, offered him the choice of three other vocations: sailor, forester or actor. It was quite a wide field to choose from, but Emil thought he would try the ocean. He may have been influenced

244

by the sight of the smart uniforms worn by sailors, but once aboard ship, he soon discovered that it was much harder work than he anticipated. One year afterwards, he succeeded in escaping from his ship and was found by a German compatriot wandering the streets of London without a cent to his name. This kindly Samaritan provided the headstrong young wanderer with enough money to get home, and Emil returned to Germany with his love of seafaring effectually quenched. It would appear that he never seriously considered forestry as his life work, for we find him next embarked upon a stage career.

At the age of sixteen, he received his first engagement at the Görlitz City Theatre, thus beginning his twelve years of acting with stock companies. It was an arduous preparation, but a good one, for he says himself, "I played everything placed in my hands." "Everything" included rôles in "The Hunchback of Notre Dame," "Old Heidelberg," "The White Horse," "The Robbers" and many of the classic dramas which are part of the dramatic training of all aspiring actors in Germany. He received his chance to go to Berlin, the dramatic as well as the political capital of Berlin, in a curious manner. Werner Krauss, with whom Emil had once played in Nurnberg, gave so clever an imitation of him in the courtyard of the German Theatre, that he called the attention of Max Reinhardt and Felix Hollander to Emil himself, and Reinhardt at once invited him to come to Berlin. He did not appear at once at the famous Deutsches Theatre but at the Small Theatre instead. Once his apprenticeship was over, Reinhardt brought

246

him to the big playhouse, and in six months
the fame of Emil Jannings was spreading
throughout Germany. He won his reputation by his splendid acting in the better
known works of Ibsen, Shakespeare, Schil-
ler and Goethe, and for eight years he
loomed large in the annals of the German
theatrical world.

In 1915, after a great deal of persuasion,
Emil Jannings consented to play in motion
pictures. His first attempts, in short films,
did not predispose him in favor of the
artistic possibilities of this new form of entertainment, and it was only by dint of the
most strenuous persuasion that Ernst Lubitsch won his consent to appear in "Du
Barry," released in this country as "Passion." Anyone who saw that remarkable
picture, in which Pola Negri gave her best
performance, will recall the splendid work

of Emil Jannings in the rôle of Louis XV. When the film was brought over to America, there were no names attached, only Miss Negri's was made known, and that was because she was already being considered as a prospect for American pictures. It was impossible to overlook Emil Jannings, however, and the next German films which he made—he had by this time given up his stage work to appear in pictures alone— were sold quite as much on his name as on their own merits. Among the most famous of these early efforts were "Deception," in which he portrayed Henry VIII, "The Loves of Pharaoh," in which he was Pharaoh, "Peter the Great," "Danton" and "Othello." These remarkable historical or semi-historical pictures, made a tremendous sensation at the time, and for sheer pictorial and dramatic effect, are still remembered

248

as outstanding films of their kind.

Four other films Jannings was to make before he left Germany for the United States. Unquestionably the most famous was "The Last Laugh," but it has a close rival in "Variety." The other two were "Tartuffe" and "Quo Vadis," in the latter of which he played the Emperor Nero. All four of these pictures were released in this country, but the first two attracted the most attention. "The Last Laugh" was directed by Frederick Murnau, and found Emil Jannings in the first of his now famous portrayals of middle-aged men, whose lives are wrecked by some apparently slight circumstance, and who go from the heights of contentment to the depths of misery. On this first occasion, he played a hotel doorman, proud as a peacock of his gorgeous uniform, who is demoted to the men's washroom

249

when his strength begins to go and suffers agonies in losing the outward appearance of splendor. This film had two endings, one logical, the other fantastically happy for the sake of the tender-hearted foreign public. Jannings himself, being a believer in stern realism, had no use for sweetness and light when they falsified the whole purpose of the preceding story. "Variety," almost equally remarkable a piece of work, was notable for the amazingly acrobatic photography and the sense of doom with which the director impregnated a comparatively simple triangle drama of circus life. Jannings took the part of Boss Huller, a great hulk of an acrobat, who deserted his wife to run away with a circus performer, and when he found her faithless, killed her lover with his bare hands and gave himself up to the police. The overwhelming agony, the mounting fury and the silent purposefulness of the final moments are impossible to forget.

"Tartuffe" was taken fairly literally from Molière's famous satirical comedy, and Emil Jannings amused himself by portraying the sanctimonious hypocrite with lively gusto and perhaps an excess of caricature. "Quo Vadis" did not give him much opportunity, and the film appeared stilted and badly photographed by the time that it reached this country, but he gave an excellent portrayal of the vain, amorous, near-sighted brutal emperor of such appalling reputation.

In 1922 Emil Jannings married Gussie Holl, a German vaudeville actress, known on the Continent as the "Elsie Janis of Germany." She is small, bobbed-haired and smartly dressed. They have one child, a

251

daughter, Ruth. His tremendous success at home, coupled with his fear of crossing the ocean, caused Emil Jannings to resist the offers made him by American film producers over a period of ten years. He made a remark on the subject that is worth repeating: urged to come to the United States, because he could earn more money than was possible in Germany, he said, "I do not eat gold-plated beefsteak, and I have no use for more than two limousines at a time." Finally, however, he was won over and agreed to sign a contract with Paramount for a certain number of films to be made in this country. So anxious was the company to obtain his services that all sorts of concessions were made: he was granted permission to choose his own stories and to have his scenes photographed in chronological order, not, as was the prevailing

Emil Jannings

custom, according to the convenience of the scene builder. Not even these concessions, however, could induce him to sign for more than a year. When asked what kind of a house he would like, the only stipulation that he made was that it should be large, and the one chosen for him was not unlike the White House, so far as size was concerned.

On October 18, 1926, Emil Jannings landed in New York. The only American words that he knew were "Good Night" and "Good Morning," nor did he manifest the slightest interest in acquiring a knowledge of the English language. Arrived in Hollywood, he went to his new house at once. The climate was much too warm and sunny to suit him and only on rainy days did he really feel at home. Worse than that, however, was the loneliness: for until

253

he could discover enough German expatriates to form a nucleus of friends, he felt like a child that has wandered into a large and unfriendly gathering. Social life did not appeal to him, and he did not care for large, fashionable parties, preferring to entertain his German friends in his own home, where they could eat German food, sing German songs and pretend that they were back in Germany. Things seemed very strange to him for a time, and it is quite possible that when the time came for him to return to Germany—with the arrival of talking pictures—he did not regret it altogether.

In the studios he worked hard and carefully, no whit daunted by the fact that all the conversation had to be carried on through an interpreter, save in the event that he had a German-speaking director.

254

Not by any means a complicated person and being possessed of a rather childlike nature, he won a great deal of affection in spite of his sporadic fits of temperament. He was obviously proud of his abilities but in a naïve, expansive fashion that never caused offence. Fond of praise, anxious to be liked, nothing gave him more pleasure than to be recognized on the street by some screen enthusiast. Perhaps his ability to assume characters so far outside his own experience rests in part upon the essential simplicity of his own nature. In repose, his face is much younger than you might think, and he has very few lines save in his forehead. His eyes are brown, his thinning hair a light tan. At one time he tipped the scales at a mere three hundred pounds, but it never worried him in the least, for he always dressed in the most conspicuous manner

possible, choosing brightly colored suits
large and showy cars, chairs and houses.
The only small thing about him was his
fondness for tiny, gold-tipped cigarettes.

His first American picture was "The
Way of All Flesh," the story of a prosperous business man who falls prey to a schem-
ing woman whom he meets on a journey.
The plot was sordid and ended on a dreary
note, but it was undoubtedly a success. Jannings himself spoke of it as a variation on
the "King Lear theme," which he believes
to be the keynote of all his recent impersonations. His many years of training in the
theatre and of rehearsing under the most
difficult circumstances, stood him in good
stead in the film studios, for he could work
quite as obliviously on a set crowded with
persons watching him as he could when
quite alone. Those who took part in his

films observed with keen interest the skill with which he sank his own personality into that of the character which he was portraying, and how, after taking the part of an old man before the camera, he would leave the set with bent head and shuffling walk.

Undoubtedly the most famous of the films which Jannings made during his sojourn in Hollywood were "The Patriot" and "The Last Command." The others were "Street of Sin," a gloomy and slightly improbable drama of the reformation and death of a gang leader in the Limehouse district of London; "Sins of the Fathers," in which he played a simple German restaurant owner who rises to be a bootlegger on a huge scale—it was in this picture that he persuaded Ruth Chatterton to make her screen debut—and "Betrayal," a slow-moving story of a Swiss peasant, agonized by the

257

death of his wife and the discovery that one of his adored children is not his own. This was his last American made picture and bore unmistakable signs of hasty workmanship in every respect save that of the star's acting, which had all the deliberateness and emotional power of his former work.

Both "The Last Command" and "The Patriot" were Russian in subject. The former told of the adventures of a proud Russian general, overwhelmed by the Revolution, who finds his way to Hollywood as an extra, his mind half destroyed by the shock of past experiences. Fate puts him under the direction of a man, formerly a revolutionist, who had always hated him. The latter tries to humiliate the broken-down Czarist officer by putting him in a film in which he would be forced to reenact some of his past life, but the scheme goes awry: the general's mind is restored sufficiently so that he believes the make-believe real and dies convinced that he has led his forces to victory to the strains of the Russian national anthem. Melodramatic and improbable as the story was, it was acted with such fire and such pathos by Jannings—indeed, by all the players—that it left an unforgettable impression. In very different key was "The Patriot," the story of the death of Paul, the mad Czar of Russia, as the result of a conspiracy headed by the one man in the world whom he trusted, Count Pahlen, minister of war. The picture was directed by Lubitsch and stirred up an infinite amount of controversy. In this country it was hailed as a masterpiece, and Jannings' impersonation of the repulsive, beast-like Paul considered a marvelous

259

piece of acting. In Europe, on the other hand, many felt that it was an undue distortion of history and that Jannings was guilty of melodramatic, unwarranted excess. None the less, it was a powerful piece of work, in which Jannings was forced to share the honors with that fine and resourceful player, Lewis Stone, who fairly surpassed himself in the rôle of Pahlen.

With his splendid record of successful and interesting pictures, it seemed incredible that anything could put a stop to Jannings' American screen work, but in 1929 arose the specter of talking pictures and soon the great German actor found that he was no longer indispensable. Returning to Germany, he found himself cordially welcomed and set to work at once to repair the omission that had cost him so much. The English language was by no means an easy hurdle to take, but he persevered, and in the summer of 1930, he set to work on "The Blue Angel," his first talking film. Since this picture was intended to re-establish him as firmly in talking films as he was in silent pictures, it was necessary for him to appear in both the German and the English versions. Speech in itself did not bother him, for unlike many American players, he had been accustomed to speaking his lines in silent films. When "The Blue Angel" was released in Europe, it proved enormously successful, despite the threadbare subject matter and depressing atmosphere of the story. Jannings, once more working on his "King Lear theme," played a respectable professor whose infatuation for a cheap cabaret singer drags him down to the depths. Marlene Dietrich played the singer, and her reputation was made by her remarkable

261

work. Late in the autumn of 1930, the picture reached America, and raised hopes, by its success, that Jannings would soon return. His English, while pronouncedly accented, was quite understandable, and his acting was as fine as it had always been. Paramount planned to bring him back in the spring of this year, but nothing has been settled as yet.

With "The Blue Angel" a success Emil Jannings decided to try his hand at his first love once more and go back to the stage for a while. This return proved to be a highly sentimental and exciting occasion. His play was Octave Mirabeau's *"Les Affaires Sont les Affaires,"* and so wild was the excitement that he received fifty curtain calls on the opening night, was bombarded with bouquets and had to be guarded by the police while entering and leaving the theatre to save him from hysterical admirers. While this proves without question that his popularity on the Continent is undiminished, it would also appear to indicate that audiences in this country would be glad to have him back. There seems to be no valid reason why Emil Jannings should not return to this country and make more pictures if he so desires. There is no one to take his place; there is no one who can even faintly approach him. Surely some way might be found to have him do a certain amount of work here, even though he prefers to spend the majority of his time in Germany. He has a lot to teach us that we should be only too glad to learn.

TOM MIX

THERE are two classes of people to whom Tom Mix, greatest of the cowboy actors, makes his special appeal. First and most important, the children adore him, flock to see him and hang on his every gesture and word. Second, members of the press find him one of the easiest persons they have ever had to interview. Picturesque, verging even on the flamboyant, he wears brilliant clothes and two-gallon hats and talks with the utmost fluency about himself and his work. The pictures in which he has played are laid chiefly in the great outdoors, and Tom has acquired a largeness of gesture and freedom of manner that have as a natural source the surroundings in which he usually finds himself. His

fondness for high-heeled boots, gaily decorated, is not an affectation but the natural
result of having worn that sort of footgear
most of his life. At fifty-two, he is as wiry
and active as he was at twenty-five, and
there seem to be no bounds to his energy
and enthusiasm. Having abandoned films
three years ago, he is now coming back,
after much urging, and his public is waiting
for him with an eagerness that borders on
impatience.

Born in El Paso, Texas, on January 6,
1880, Tom Mix has led a life in which romance, excitement, adventure and hard
work all have a share. From his earliest
childhood, he claims a deep interest in Wild
West shows, for he used to get up before
dawn in order to see the train bearing Col.
William Cody, the immortal Buffalo Bill,
and his company pass through the town.

Soon, however, he found merely the suggestion of adventure too tame to satisfy him, and before he was twenty, he had taken service as one of Theodore Roosevelt's "Rough Riders" and thus found himself in the midst of the Spanish American War. He also served as a member of the Grimes Battery in the Santiago campaign, where he supplemented his knowledge of gunnery and acquired the ability to shoot straight, which was to stand him in such good stead in his future occupations. Many would have considered one war sufficient for a lifetime, but for him it was not enough and therefore, at the close of hostilities, Tom went further afield, to Africa, to be exact, and fought for the English in the Boer War.

Possibly the United States may have seemed a bit tame to the restless Mr. Mix

266

when he returned home after his soldiering, but he found that in Oklahoma life was still reasonably primitive, so he betook himself thither in all haste and once arrived, seized upon the most active sort of work he could find. He began as a ranger and then became in turn sheriff and marshal. Thirty years ago, Oklahoma was not quite as civilized as it is now, and young Sheriff Mix was undoubtedly concerned in much the same sort of adventures which he has portrayed so many times and with such convincing verisimilitude on the screen. He took a fling at motion pictures quite early in his career and looked upon them as silly. There was too much wild riding and shouting and gesticulation in films, he decided, and when a bandit chief in Mexico by the name of Madero offered him five hundred dollars to catch some of his enemies, Tom thought it far more sensible. He went to Mexico and managed to capture the men and collect his pay. More than that, he obtained five followers and so became a captain. If he had had fifty, he says that he could have been a general.

The five hundred dollars lasted quite a while, but when that was spent he had to support himself and his four horses by performing tricks with a lariat in the streets of small Texas towns and passing the hat afterwards. He managed to live in this manner, but it wasn't too satisfactory, so when another motion picture offer came his way, he accepted it without asking any questions. He was told to report at the Selig studios in Chicago where a pretentious two-reeler was in progress. All that he had to do was double for the leading man and kill a few wolves with his bare hands. They shut

268

Tom up in a small room and sent the wolves in by the window. Tom seized the largest of the pack, by the hind legs, unfortunately, and after annihilating the room completely, Tom believed that the beast was dead. So did everyone else, including the leading man who stepped into the picture and placed one foot on the wolf's head in an off-hand manner. The wolf, nevertheless, was still alive and came to so unexpectedly that the leading man promptly fainted dead away. Tom was given one hundred dollars for this little job, but as half of this went to pay his fine with the S. P. C. A. and most of the rest in treatment for wolf bites, Tom's opinion of films became even lower than before.

Dangerous "stunt" riding, trick shooting and a variety of hazardous exploits have always been part of the day's work for Tom

Mix. He has never had a double in his life, and as a result has spent a considerable amount of time in the hospital. One difficult, though not especially dangerous, task that he was given was the killing of buffalo. Tom is a good shot, but a buffalo is not easy to bring down at full gallop. The first time he tried it, he was unable to find a vulnerable spot, until someone suggested aiming for the spot where the spinal cord joins the neck at the base of the animal's skull. This proved as effective as the old-time hunters' method of severing the jugular vein, and Tom soon found himself in the papers on account of his remarkable marksmanship.

Once launched in films with Selig—it is likely that the wolf episode won him considerable attention—Tom began to get regular work and soon found, once leading rôles started to come his way, that it was by no means a bad way to earn a living. Even growing fame, fortunately, could not make him let up on his efforts to keep fit, for his rôles were of the sort that kept him in action practically without respite. Riding, running, jumping—chiefly on and off horseback—accurate shooting and similar strenuous activities made it imperative that he should keep alert and steady. As part of his daily training he boxed as much as possible and watched his diet so carefully that for twenty years he varied little in weight.

Selig may have launched Tom Mix, but it was with Fox Films that he won his great reputation and made the majority of his pictures. His fan mail reached tremendous proportions, and being both far-sighted and businesslike, he went through this with great care. For the majority of his admirers, an autographed picture of himself

271

was enough of a reply, but when it came to doctors, lawyers and clergymen he adopted another plan. Realizing that these men were of influence and importance in their communities, Tom used to write to them, saying how much he appreciated their interest and how glad he would be of any suggestions or criticisms that they might care to offer. He kept a card index in which were arranged methodically all the different sorts of stories in which he had appeared, with notations on each card concerning the prevalence of public opinion on each one. If one may judge by the type of films in which he has appeared most often, what his public demanded was plenty of action, a simple plot, a very white hero, a very black villain, one or two dastardly schemes to be foiled and a helpless, clinging-vine heroine to be rescued at the last possible moment.

This sort of picture has been popular since motion pictures first began, and is likely to hold its place indefinitely.

These films were not hard to make and called for simple costumes and comparatively little scenery outside that supplied by nature and some simple frame buildings. Of course, horses were needed, for Tom Mix without a horse would be a worse anomaly than a circus without an elephant, for, like the hero in the absurd but apt quotation, Tom was forever "vaulting into the saddle and riding off in all directions."

Since 1910, his favorite mount and almost inseparable companion has been Tony, whom he bought when a colt and trained himself. Even when Tom Mix owned as many as a hundred horses, Tony has been the one for which the public clamored. He is a beautiful animal, extremely intelligent,

273

and, despite his years, has always been so well treated that he was able to appear with his master during the latter's three season engagement with the Sells-Floto Circus.

Among the early films in which Tom Mix appeared for Fox are the following: "Cupid's Round Up," "The Queen of Sheba," "A Ridin' Romeo," "Rough Riding Romance," "The Feud," "The Texan," "Chasing the Moon," "Up and Going," "The Fighting Streak," "For Big Stakes," "Just Tony," "Do and Dare," "Tom Mix in Arabia," "Romance Land," "Catch My Smoke," "Three Jumps Ahead," "Soft Boiled," "Drums of Arabia," and many more. Most of these, as the titles indicated, were romances of the old west, the west of cattle-punchers, boom towns, quick shootings, deeds of daring with a minimum of subtitles. Tom preferred the riding to the

Tom Mix

love-making, and found his style decidedly
cramped when called upon to kiss a pretty
girl. The public didn't mind his reluc-
tance for sentimental scenes, for he gave
them what they asked for: action and still
more action. Western dramas may be
crude, they may be improbable, but so long
as they keep moving, and moving fast,
audiences won't stop to ask questions about
probability. Talking films, far from dimin-
ishing their popularity, seem to have in-
creased it.

With every film he made, Tom Mix's
popularity grew, and with his popularity
and the demand for his pictures, so did his
salary increase until rumor placed it, in
1925, at twenty thousand dollars a week.
Be that as it may, by 1921 Tom thought
he would retire and live on his earnings.
He was a very rich man, he had made the

equivalent of several fortunes, and he did not see any reason why he should keep on working. Perhaps he might have carried out this threat, had not the love and admiration of his youthful film "fans" persuaded him that the time to stop had not yet come. They wrote to him continually, they worshipped him openly on the streets, and they loved his pictures to such an extent that retirement finally appeared to him both as a cruel trick to play on the youngsters and an unwise business proposition as well. To be sure, he didn't really need the money, but he did enjoy the work. It is not likely that he had cause to regret this decision, for he has been welcomed by young and old alike in all the towns he visited with such affection as is accorded to very few.

It is to be regretted Tom Mix has not had the same good fortune in his private life as he has in his professional career. He has been twice married and twice divorced, and owing to his fame, the divorces have brought him more publicity than may have been altogether agreeable. His first marriage ended in the courts during the year 1917, and his wife, Olive Stokes, was given the custody of their only child, Ruth Jane, born in 1912. The following year he married Victoria Forde. She later divorced him in 1930, after an attempted reconciliation had failed to proceed harmoniously. His second child, Tomasina, was born in 1922.

The public has always been loyal to him, however, and flocked whole-heartedly to the generous yearly quota of pictures that he turned out. In 1926, he completed seven: "The Yankee Senor," "Tony Runs Wild," "My Own Pal," "Hardboiled,"

"The Great K and A Robbery," "The Canyon of Light," and "No Man's Gold." The following year brought seven more. "The Last Trail," "The Broncho Twister," "The Outlaws of Red River," "The Circus Ace," "Tumbling River," "Silver Valley," and "The Arizona Wildcat." These adventure yarns were succeeded by a like number for the year 1928. Included among them were "The Devil's Reward," "A Horseman of the Plains," "Hello, Cheyenne," "Painted Post," and "A Son of the Golden West." In 1929, he made three films only: "Outlawed," "The Big Diamond Robbery," and "The Drifter." With these completed, Tom Mix turned his back on motion pictures, apparently for good, and entered the more lucrative field of the circus, having accepted a handsome contract from Sells-Floto. Before it went into

278

effect, however, he undertook a vaudeville tour, taking with him the popular Tony, and two cowboys to assist him in the lariat work. The tour was a great success, both the star and his horse proving as much at home on the comparatively narrow confines of the stage as they had on the open plains.

It was a curious coincidence that Tom Mix, twenty years ago, should have played with the Sells-Floto Circus, but then he was only an unknown cowboy, who received the large sum of twenty dollars a week for trick riding. This time he went in state as the star attraction, with a private car for himself, another one for Tony, with a retinue of actors and servants, and receiving the princely sum of twenty thousand dollars a week. Everywhere the circus went, Tom Mix drew the crowds, and he made positively triumphant progress all over the country. For the edification of the crowds, he proved that time had robbed him of none of his suppleness and daring, and he performed all sorts of spectacular and hazardous feats. When comment was made on the size of his weekly recompense, he replied: "I'm not afraid of hard work, but I must have my comforts." For three seasons, until October of this year, in fact, Tom Mix remained with the circus, despite the efforts of the manager of a well-known Wild West show to detach him on the basis of a previous contract.

Last May, the news was made known that Tom Mix was returning to films, having left them at the time when talking pictures were crowding silent dramas from the screen. Of course, there had been rumors to that effect before, but this time it was a certainty. Universal Pictures had obtained his signature to a contract calling for six pictures, and he had agreed to start work in the autumn. By that time, the circus would have reached Los Angeles on its cross-country tour, and after playing under the big tent for the last time, he would return to the bright lights of the studios and become a screen actor once more. By the middle of the summer, his first vehicle had been decided upon: a story by Courtney Riley Cooper entitled: "Christmas Eve at Pilot Butte," which has the sound of a fast-moving, satisfactorily sentimental melodrama—just the sort of thing to bring back the cowboy star.

At the present time, there seems every reason to believe that Tom Mix will find his popularity with his huge public unaltered during the months of his absence. Now that people all over the country have

281

seen him in person and realize that there is no make-believe about his horsemanship, it is likely that he will be even more popular than ever.

No matter how great has been his fame, how fabulous his bank-account, Tom Mix has always worked hard. For the last few years he has made pictures and done his circus riding with one shoulder held together by wire, while injuries to his spine have caused him considerable pain and frequent visits to a hospital. Perhaps this has contributed to make him particularly sympathetic and friendly with the crippled children whom he so often entertains, but however you look at it, it has taken plenty of pluck to go on under these conditions. Whatever may be one's opinion of his acting—and he has never made any great pretentions on that score—few can resist the fascination of watching a man on horse-back, who is so completely at one with his animal, so sure of himself, so graceful and easy. The old West has passed, but Tom Mix can still persuade youngsters of today of its zestful and exciting possibilities, and prove to them that a horse has more per-sonality than an automobile.

This promised return to the screen, over which there had been so many happy ex-pectations, was nearly cut short for good and all when Mr. Mix, on the eve of starting work on his first new film, was stricken with an attack of appendicitis which rapidly de-veloped into peritonitis. For several days his life was despaired of, but he made a gal-lant fight and to the amazement and delight of his hordes of admirers was finally pro-nounced out of danger.

WILLIAM POWELL

CHANGES occur rapidly in motion pictures, but the variations in the character of William Powell's rôles during the last two and a half years have been the most complete in filmdom. Mr. Powell has been in films since 1922, and until the coming of talking-pictures played a practically unbroken series of desperate characters. In the story he was the sort of person whom no one could trust for a moment, and yet he was never quite the conventional villain. Perhaps this ability to vary his rôles has been the secret of his ascent to stardom and, consequently, to sympathetic rôles.

Seven seasons in unpleasant rôles, seven years of nefarious plots and evil-doing, would make any man long for a change, but the surprising fact is the equanimity with which the public accepts Mr. Powell's change of status. Usually an actor is pigeon-holed quite as much by the fans as by the studios, and if he deviates from the ex-pected part, there is apt to be an outcry. William Powell, curious to say, has risen from the lowest and most dastardly of vil-lains to playing sympathetic, even noble parts, from the background to the center of the stage, and his progress has met with universal acclaim. This is indeed a pleas-ing symptom, for Mr. Powell is the sort of person who plays every part with intelli-gence, no matter how small or how large it happens to be. Having to make up in some respect for his irregularity of features, he chose to use his brains, since his profile was out of the question. It was probably his

285

face that caused him to take up the acting of such villainous parts, for in the early days of films, one could not be a hero unless he was handsome. With all the accusations that may still justly be hurled against films today, that ancient fetish has been disposed of, on the masculine side, at least. Nowadays, our best screen players are not those most noticeable for their good looks: George Arliss, Emil Jannings, Walter Huston, Wallace Beery, Douglas Fairbanks, and William Powell being among the more notable examples. All these men are extremely popular, more so than many of the younger and handsomer players. Maturity, bringing with it poise acquired by experience, adds to, rather than detracts from the interest aroused by their work.

Like many screen players, whose acting bespeaks years of growth and practice, Wil-

286

liam Powell was born, not to the screen world, but to the theatre. The place of his birth was Pittsburgh and the date July 29, 1893. He believes that from the cradle on he was destined to be an actor, for his mother once told him that he started making speeches almost before he could talk. She first thought he might become an orator, but later modified her decision in favor of the law. The future screen star, christened William Horatio Powell, spent the first fourteen years of his life in Pittsburgh, after which he moved to Kansas City with his family and entered the Central High School. While in school, he took up acting with the dramatic society, but his efforts were not greeted with much enthusiasm at home. With the dramatic fire burning in his veins, he longed to go to New York and study at a dramatic school, but his parents could not afford to send him, nor did they approve of the idea. When he graduated from school in 1911, he realized that in order to get his dramatic training he would need seven hundred dollars for one year's tuition and expenses. The only thing for William to do then, was to earn the money to educate himself. Accordingly, he went to work for the Home Telephone Company at a salary of fifty dollars a month, intending to save all his money by living at home.

For one reason or another this excellent scheme did not bear fruit. In desperation William wrote a twenty-three page letter to a rich and eccentric aunt, begging her to lend him the necessary funds with which to go to New York and study. Her response was favorable. In the late summer William packed his bag, took the train for New York where he enrolled at the famous

American Academy of Dramatic Art, founded in 1884 by the late Franklin H. Sargent. After a year of schooling, he sought for an opportunity to try out the results of his study. Presently he found an opening which would just about supply him with a week's food, and then he received a small assignment in "The Ne'er-Do-Well," a play taken by Charles Klein from Rex Beach's story. The play did not last long, however, and after two weeks William was again tramping the streets looking for work. Finally, after a winter which he describes as the hardest he ever spent, he was given the rôle of Eddie Griggs in "Within the Law," an engagement which lasted for two years.

Much of this time, however, was spent on tour, although the young actor was anxious to make a name for himself on

Broadway. Realizing the need for a thorough training and wide experience, he undertook stock company work. For four seasons he played all sorts of parts with companies in Pittsburgh, Portland, Oregon; Detroit, Buffalo, Northampton and Worcester, acquiring a wide knowledge of the theatre. At the end of this period of voluntary apprenticeship, he obtained a part that promised to lead him back to New York. This play was "The King" with Leo Dietrichstein as star. William's part was so small that he did not leave any particular impression on the great metropolis. The next season, though you may find it hard to believe, he went in for musical comedy and supported Frank Craven in "Going Up," taken from the popular comedy, "The Aviator." This was followed by a year in Boston with the Castle Square stock company

under John Craig. In 1919 he returned to
New York to try his luck again. For a
time this proved to be persistently bad. He
obtained engagements in five plays, every
one of which failed before it reached New
York.

Finally he was given a really good part
in a romantic melodrama, "Spanish Love,"
by Avery Hopwood and Mary Roberts
Rinehart, which had its New York première
at the Maxine Elliott Theatre on August 17,
1920. This time William achieved his ambition and was very much noticed by the
reviewers. One of them said: "The son of
William H. Powell, wracked in body, heart,
and mind, had the sting of reality"; another
one remarked, "William H. Powell did
valiant work as the man who was dying
hard"; and there was even a short bio-
graphical article about him in the New

York Times. In those days he still kept the H. in his name. It was the attention he received from his portrayal in "Spanish Love" of the unhappy youth who is fatally wounded by the sweetheart of the girl he loves, that brought William his first motion picture offers. Previously he had tried to enter films without success, and now he had the pleasure of refusing to accept offers from screen producers.

Finally he decided to accept the rôle of Fortman in the Metro production of "Sherlock Holmes" in which John Barrymore was starred. After this he alternated between stage and screen, until the fall of 1922 when Richard Barthelmess asked him to come to Cuba and take part in his production of Hergesheimer's "The Bright Shawl." His last appearance on the stage was in a play called "The Woman Who

Laughed," by Edward Locke, which opened at the Longacre Theatre in New York on August 16, 1922 and closed there two weeks later. His engagement with Richard Barthelmess led to a warm friendship.

Following "The Bright Shawl," William Powell appeared in a number of well-known productions, among which were "When Knighthood Was in Flower," "Under the Red Robe," "Romola," (with Lillian Gish and Ronald Colman), "Too Many Kisses," and "Outcast." His rôles were not very important, but he made a conscientious effort to distinguish between them and impart to each an individuality not usually found in minor parts. The longer he stayed in films, the more interested he became in trying to build up the background of each character that he was given to play, in order that he might understand exactly how this character would behave in any given set of circumstances. This is the quality which makes so many of his characterizations to-day seem snatched from real life; it is as though the camera had caught glimpses of these men as they went about their daily life, not as though they were just puppets taking on a brief existence for the purposes of an imaginary story. He said once that, so far as he was concerned, "—some of the characters I have portrayed seem like old friends now, because of the intimate details of their lives that I have built up in my own imagination."

In the year 1926 William Powell appeared in a number of pictures of varying importance, among them "Sea Horses," "White Mice," "Desert Gold," "The Runaway," "Aloma of the South Seas," (with Warner Baxter and Gilda Gray), "Great

William Powell

Gatsby," "Tin Gods," and "Beau Geste."
Of these the last is unquestionably the most
famous, and even with the unusually large
number of excellent characterizations by
other prominent actors Mr. Powell's work
made a memorable impression. He took
the unlovely part of an Italian thief, Boldini
by name, who attempts to steal the supposed
diamond from Michael Geste, is drastically
punished and ends his life ingloriously trying to laugh at death from the watch tower
of a besieged fort in the Arabian desert.
This picture put the actor high up on the
list of what may be described as "picture
stealers"—in other words, those supposedly
subsidiary players who distract attention
from the stars.

During the following season he again
played in a variety of productions, among
them numerous comedies. He played with

Bebe Daniels in "She's a Sheik," and in "Senorita." Others on the list were "New York," "Love's Greatest Mistake," "Special Delivery," "Time to Love," "Paid to Love," and "Nevada." None of these productions was especially notable, but the name of William Powell was kept continually before the public in preparation for his remarkable leap to fame which was to be made during 1928. Among the films of this momentous year were "Beau Sabreur," "Feel My Pulse," "Partners in Crime," "The Dragnet," "The Vanishing Pioneer," "Forgotten Faces," "The Last Command," and "Interference." "Beau Sabreur" was the disappointing follow-up of "Beau Geste," "Feel My Pulse," a comedy-melodrama, and "The Vanishing Pioneer," a Western drama. "Partners in Crime" proved to be an exciting melodrama of the underworld

and "The Dragnet," in which William
Powell played with George Bancroft, Evelyn Brent, and Fred Kohler, was an even
more interesting film, giving Mr. Powell
the chance to play the rôle of a smooth
criminal in a decidedly striking fashion.
"Forgotten Faces" was a sordid but striking
drama of an unpleasant woman whose husband is forced to kill her to prevent her
from ruining their daughter's life.

"The Last Command" and "Interference," the opening and closing of that season, deserve special mention. The former
was a powerful, intensely dramatic drama
in which a Russian general, losing everything in the Revolution, drifts to Hollywood
where he finds himself acting as extra in a
picture directed by a certain revolutionist
whom he had once sentenced to prison after
a violent quarrel. Emil Jannings acted the

part of the general, William Powell the revolutionist and they played together marvelously. Mr. Powell's depiction of the man,
once despised and abused, who seizes the
supreme chance to be revenged upon the
man whom he hated, finally remorseful at
the overwhelming success of his ingenious
plan. His tribute of greatness of the pitiful
old man whom he had caused to die in a last
delusion of greatness, was remarkably fine,
filled with skillful touches and bits of subtle
suggestion that built up a well rounded and
striking figure. "Interference," the first
talking picture in which William Powell
played, succeeded definitely in establishing
him as a coming star. His excellent voice,
his smooth, polished manner, and easy as-
sumption of emotion masked under flippant
cynicism, made him the outstanding person
in a cast that included Clive Brook, Evelyn

Brent, and Doris Kenyon. Coming at a time when those players who were at ease before the microphone found themselves in constant demand, William Powell's reputation skyrocketed to the heights.

The Paramount studios, to which he had been under contract for several years, decided to make him a star and selected for his first vehicle one of the popular S. S. Van Dine mystery stories. This was "The Canary Murder Case" in which William Powell was presented to a highly approving public in the guise of Philo Vance, the super-detective, who cultivated the arts and at the same time concealed an infernally clever mind under the exterior of a dilettante connoisseur. The picture was a success, although the star had little to do but walk through his part and speak a number of interesting lines in his pleasingly modulated

voice. It was followed by "The Greene
Murder Case," a grimly fantastic murder
story by Mr. Van Dine, in which Mr.
Powell once more as Vance was given far
more satisfying opportunities. Not all the
year, however, was spent in detective stories,
for the actor appeared, in rapid succession,
in "The Four Feathers," "Charming Sin-
ners," "Behind the Makeup," and "Pointed
Heels." The first was taken from a novel
by A. E. W. Mason which told of the re-
demption of a man accused of cowardice;
the second was a clever and amusing adaptation of Somerset Maugham's play, "The
Constant Wife," a highly entertaining picture in which Mr. Powell took the rôle of
the hopeful lover of a self-contained and
charming wife who first aids her husband
in his love affairs and then decides to amuse
herself. "Behind the Make-Up" presented

Mr. Powell in the ungrateful part of a conceited vaudeville performer who falls prey to a grasping woman; "Pointed Heels" saw him as an abnormally altruistic and improbable theatrical producer.

The year 1930 brought William Powell a number of unusually interesting pictures, most notable being "Street of Chance." This was the story of a brilliant man whose love of gambling exceeds all bounds, and who wrecks his own life and that of his wife as well through his weakness. In an attempt to break his younger brother of the evils of the craze, he succumbs to his former love of the game and dies in an ambulance, wagering with his last breath that he cannot live. The story, adroitly directed by John Cromwell and acted to the hilt by a splendid cast, was supposed to depict the events culminating in the recent mysterious death of a noted gambler, but made no attempt at the solution of the murder of the leading character. Next in order of interest came "For the Defence," another picture which had its foundation in real life, being derived from the career of a famous criminal lawyer. To both films Mr. Powell contributed skillfully differentiated, interesting dramatic performances that enhanced his reputation tremendously. Other pictures in which he appeared that year were "Shadow of the Law," which bore a striking resemblance to one of Thomas Meighan's silent films, "The City of Silent Men," "The Benson Murder Case" (the third and least interesting of the S. S. Van Dine mystery stories), and a brief satirical sketch in "Paramount on Parade."

Mr. Powell's first releases for the following year were "Man of the World" and

"Ladies' Man," a story which went the rounds of the studios for some time before the star decided definitely to make it. The first of these was the tale of an American expatriate who made a shady living in Paris running a scandal sheet at the expense of rich and unsuspecting Americans who paid him to have their names kept out of it. The second is the story of a man who turns his appeal to the opposite sex into hard cash by extracting handsome presents from infatuated women. His two leading ladies were Kay Francis, who had appeared with him before in "Behind the Make-Up," "Street of Chance," and "For the Defence," and Carole Lombard, a charming and intelligent young actress whom Mr. Powell married on June 26, 1931. With the completion of "Ladies' Man," his contract with Paramount came to an end, and he signed an agreement to make pictures for Warner Brothers. His first film under the new management is taken from a Roland Pertwee play, "Heat Wave."

Wherever he is, for whatever company he works, one wishes William Powell success. He has come a long road, he has worked hard, and his excellent preparation for his chosen career is demonstrated by the skill with which he projects his various rôles. He has, in fact, been in the business long enough to have an excellent idea of what it wants, both in the way of stories and of leading ladies. Not always does he find himself in agreement with the studio for which he is working, but he is apt to have a pretty good reason for what he says or does. Most important of all, for it is a thing that can be said of very few players, he always does good work, he is interesting to watch—despite his lack of masculine beauty—his acting displays authority of manner, and smoothness of touch, while his voice is one of the most cultivated and expressive of which the screen can boast.

He used to cherish one ambition of which he made no secret: to be a retired motion picture actor on the Riviera. Now that he is married and has someone else to think of besides himself, it is probable that this is no longer the case, for his avowed intention is to assist his wife in making a great career for herself. His favorite form of relaxation is sailing, a pastime in which his present popularity gives him but little time to indulge. All actors are supposed to have some unmistakable trade-mark, and William Powell's is his little moustache. Once only, for a few sequences in "Shadow of the Law," did he shave it off. Otherwise, it is

as much a part of his acting equipment as
Charlie Chaplin's derby hat and jaunty cane
are the unmistakable signs of our most
famous comedian.

WILL ROGERS

TO FEW persons is the privilege granted of becoming a legend during their own lifetimes, but Will Rogers has become as essential a portion of the American landscape as the Yellowstone Park, the National Capitol, or Niagara Falls. People read him every morning and quote him every night; they accept his political opinions with far more seriousness than those of grave and learned law-makers. They like him on the stage, they applaud him on the screen, they follow his doings with almost as much interest as though he were the Prince of Wales. It is a curious phenomenon: a middle-aged man, decidedly homely, unfashionably dressed, more of a personality than

an actor, an incessant and beguiling conversationalist, and pretty much the same whatever character he happens to be playing, yet
who can boast of fame and popularity
enough to make envious the handsomest,
most brilliant and talented of actors. Re-
garded by many as a philosopher and humorist of the first rank, he stoutly main-
tains that all he knows is what he reads
in the papers. His naïve pride in his own
ability to talk endlessly about any subject
under the sun, makes him appreciate the
full value of the occasion when he listened
to George Bernard Shaw for two hours and
a half and never uttered one word. He
firmly believes that Shaw is the only person
in the world who could have kept him still
that long.

There is probably not a more kind-
hearted soul alive, for while he pokes ridi-

cule at established men and institutions, he does it with a friendly wink that removes the sting but not the underlying truth. He can find humor in almost anything from politics to prohibition, but he never becomes personal; he does not indulge in cheap cynicism and he can make you laugh at the same time that he makes you think. It is noticeable, also, that he does not take sides on issues which cause feelings to run high: he discusses subjects that are fair game for the man on the street, but in such a manner that his listeners are apt to say to themselves that Will has an uncanny faculty of putting their thoughts into words. He moulds public opinion to the extent that presumably 40,000,000 persons follow his sayings in 350 daily and 200 Sunday newspapers from coast to coast. Will Rogers is not iconoclastic in his ideas, partly because the mere fact that he ridicules political absurdities is not remarkable. In Lincoln's time, Artemus Ward was considered almost a heretic because he dared poke fun at office-seekers and other kindred matters. Now when Will Rogers does the same thing, he is considered a humorist and not a dangerous idol-breaker.

Will was born on a ranch twelve miles north of Claremore, Indian Territory, on November 4, 1879. His claim to being descended from one of the oldest families in the neighborhood, can hardly be disputed, since his father was one-eighth Cherokee Indian and his mother had one-quarter Indian blood. Will's father was reasonably well off in addition to being a man of prominence in the community: he helped to draft the constitution under which Oklahoma finally entered the Union as a state. In recognition of his services, the county in which Clare-more is situated is called Rogers County. However, the son of a leading citizen would not stay in school for more than a few weeks at a time. He was a restless youth with a taste for adventure and experiment, both of which qualities he proved by taking a boat bound for the Argentine. For some reason, the boat went to England first and pres-ently Will found himself taking livestock to Africa for the use of the British troops then engaged in fighting the Boer war: a precari-ous living at best.

The war over, Will found himself in Africa with little to do, until an American, with the beguiling name of Texas Jack, in-vited him to do a roping act in a Wild West show in Johannesburg. This proved a satisfactory undertaking, and Will stayed with the show while it traveled around Africa from Rhodesia to Cape Town. He soon found himself a quite popular attraction and, after fourteen months, shifted his activities to the Wirth Brothers Circus in Australia. This kept him busy for six months, at the end of which period he came to San Francisco. Hearing that the St. Louis World's Fair was about to start, he traveled eastward and joined another Wild West show that was held on the grounds. Then in his late twenties, he was a good example of the many cowboys who found it more lucrative to wear their chaps, embroidered boots and wide sombreros before the footlights than to waste their time riding the ranges. The stage offered them less work and more money, a combination which they made little effort to resist. Once and again—this was back in 1904—they would drift into motion picture work and make

the Wild West pictures that proved so pop-
ular in the early days of the film industry.
It was not the screen, however, that brought
Will his first introduction to fame.

Some enterprising manager had an idea
that Will could do well in a steer-roping
act on the stage. By 1905, he was doing this
very thing at Hammerstein's Victoria Theatre and other less important houses. Gradually the spirit of economy suggested that
the steer be eliminated as too expensive an
item, and Will walked on to the stage alone
to twirl a rope. His skill with the lariat
made him popular even in those days, but he
became almost too good. The manager of
the Union Square Theatre in New York,
explained to Will that while his act was
good, the inhabitants of Fourteenth Street
could hardly be expected to know what
rope-twirling was all about, and hinted that

a few words of explanation might not come amiss. The moment Will opened his mouth, the audience roared with delight over what they considered his ludicrous Oklahoma dialect, which made the future long-distance conversationalist so angry that he threatened to leave the show on the spot. He insisted that he was not trying to be funny and did not care to be an object of mirth. It was all that the convulsed manager could do to keep him from leaving the show then and there, but finally he consented to stay on, and before long, he found himself a headliner.

At some period during the year 1913, Will attracted the attention of Florenz Ziegfeld, who needed several artists to go before the curtain and hold the attention of the audience while an elaborate backstage change of scenery was in progress. By 1914,

Will Rogers

when Will made his first appearance in the
Ziegfeld Follies, he had begun to vary his
patter about the rope-twirling with jokes,
and finally achieved outstanding success
when he tried to vary them every night. He
soon became a legend, and newspapers carried stories about him, telling how he was
able to dominate an audience of two thousand persons every evening. They even said
that he never repeated himself. Be that as
it may, he soon became an indispensable
feature of Mr. Ziegfeld's great spectacles,
and his combination of rope twirling, gum
chewing, and quizzical humor, delivered
with great seriousness—frequently from the
corner of his mouth—won him a unique
reputation.

It was due to his work in the Follies that
Will began to write for the newspapers. His
growing popularity caused him to be in con-

siderable demand as guest at big public dinners, and at one of these affairs, Louis Wiley of the New York Times, happened to be present. Mr. Wiley laughed as much as any of the guests, but he did more than laugh. He went to the news department of his paper and suggested that it might be a good idea to have some of Will's sayings incorporated in the columns of the Times. An attempt was made to have his speeches transcribed by a reporter, but it soon became evident that Will's jokes were funny only when set down in his own words. The final solution was a weekly monologue in which Will gave his own interpretation of the news of the past week. The experiment was so successful that it soon became a popular syndicated feature.

By 1915, Will Rogers was definitely a Ziegfeld star, a position which he occupied very comfortably until the coming of the eighteenth amendment put the "Ziegfeld Midnight Frolic" out of business. There were so many repeaters at this entertainment that Will had to be careful not to use the same jokes twice, and he found himself driven to reading the daily papers and extracting from them amusing ideas about various national figures, problems and jokes. Some of his audiences laughed because they thought him unsophisticated and his Oklahoma drawl very amusing. Others were entertained because he reminded them of some rural character they may have known, some village philosopher holding forth in the local store from his cracker-box throne. It is probably this genuine homely, unsophisticated flavor that keeps audiences so devoted to Will's humor; for it is genuine in its development, although considerably

317

more studied today than when he first began amusing audiences in small vaudeville
houses.

Once he found his voice on the stage,
Will found that he was much better audible
than silent. His first venture into motion
pictures took place when Mrs. Rex Beach
persuaded Samuel Goldwyn that it would
be an excellent idea to star him on the
screen, and Will made a series of six-reel
comedies that did not achieve any great
popular success. He says himself: "They
were not so hot because they were silent.
When the screen gave me a chance to talk,
I was more successful." As a pantomimist,
one can easily see how he would lose a good
deal of his appeal, although his sheepish
grin and twinkling eyes are undeniably
great assets in themselves. Among these
first silent films were "Honest Hutch,"

"Boys Will Be Boys," "Doubling For
Romeo," "The Ropin' Day," "The Head-
less Horseman," "Fruits of Faith," "Jus'
Passing Through," "Justlin' Back," "Un-
censored Movies," "Two Wagons—Both
Covered," "The Cowboy Sheik," "The
Cake Eater," "Big Moments From Little
Pictures," "Highbrow Stuff," "Going to
Congress," "A Truthful Liar," "Family
Fitz," "Jubilo, Jr.," "Our Congressman,"
"Gee Whiz, Genevieve" and a series of
shorts, entitled: "Strolling Through Europe
With Will Rogers." These were made at
the Pathé Studios. Later on he was starred
in Sam Rork's "A Texas Steer."

Three years ago, when he had just signed
a big motion picture contract, Will Rogers
went to the rescue of Fred Stone, who had
met with a terrible accident on the eve of
opening in a big new musical comedy. To

ease Fred's mind and because they had been close friends for many years, Will gave up his lucrative contract and undertook to fill Fred's place in the show, "Three Cheers." He made a great success of it, although it is reported that he gave the other members of the cast more than a few white hairs by neglecting to give them their cues at the expected moments. None the less, the show went on, and Will helped Dorothy Stone to make her stage debut. Between times, he visited Fred at the hospital and made him laugh. Mr. Stone recovered, thanks to his amazing pluck, and Will returned to the films.

This time, he was allowed to talk as much as he liked, for the sound films had come in, and producers were only too glad to find players who were not afraid to hear the sound of their own voices. His first picture, made under contract to Fox Films, was "They Had to See Paris." Wisely realizing that Will was not much of an actor, the director allowed him to improvise many of his own jokes and speak his speeches in the manner that suited him best, always providing that he followed the main outline of the story. Will was given the part of a horse-doctor from Illinois, who strikes oil in his backyard and is promptly taken to Paris by his ambitious wife in order that they may acquire poise and social prestige. He ambled cheerfully through his part, delivering his amusing lines with the same comical drawl that he used upon the stage. He never used makeup and seldom wore any sort of costume, preferring his everyday clothes. As well as his audiences, he knew that he could never alter his face or change his comedy and felt, therefore, that it would be futile to attempt any manner of disguise.

The picture proved popular, even though it was practically all a monologue by Will, and he was soon put to work on another; this being "So This Is London," an entertaining comedy of Anglo-American misunderstandings, based somewhat distantly upon the successful stage play of the same name. Will appeared as a shrewd Yankee business man who distrusted everything English until he went to visit in an English country house and had a delightful time. Unmistakably himself, he wandered happily around the sets, speaking lines that were as unexpected as they were funny. Particularly amusing was the scene in which he tried to act like the Indian brave that his hide-bound host expected him to be—sliding down the banisters, executing a war dance in the hall just before dinner and uttering various guttural whoops that were supposed to be Indian dialect.

Next came "Lightnin'," a mild little comedy that Frank Bacon made famous all over the country. Will had the time of his life playing the meek good-for-nothing husband of the enterprising Reno hotel keeper. It was the first screen rôle that gave him definite opportunities for consistent characterization, and he did splendid work as the shrewd, honest, dawdling man, cleverer than he looked, affectionate and simple-hearted, smart enough to save his wife's property and regain her affection and respect. It was always a good play, and while Will bore little or no resemblance to Frank Bacon, he achieved considerable success. The picture was well acted throughout. In one of the smaller rôles, George M. Cohan's daughter, Helen, made her screen debut.

Though Will has never made any pretense at being anything but an Oklahoman, Fox Films thought that he was the very person to take the leading rôle in their picturization of Mark Twain's "A Connecticut Yankee at King Arthur's Court." While Will is no Yankee, he had a beautiful time as the bewildered Hank Peters who found himself suddenly transported back into the sixth century. His humor was his own, rather than Mark Twain's, but the spirit was the same, and the resulting film proved laughable in the extreme. The author's conception was partly serious, along with its ludicrous moments, but Will was content to be humorous throughout. In a suit of armour, he made a most absurd appearance, resembling nothing so much as a mechanical doll. To see him lassoing the knights on the tournament field, saving himself at the stake by means of a lucky eclipse of the sun, turning the palace into a gigantic factory and sending the king's army out to battle in a fleet of miniature automobiles, was excellent foolery.

"A Connecticut Yankee" was Will's first release for 1931, and he followed it with a George Ade story, originally entitled, "Father and Boys," then christened, "Cure for the Blues" and finally released as "Young As You Feel." This time, contrary to his custom, Will had to dress up, and convulsed spectators by appearing in a full-dress suit and very English sporting attire. With that done, he started work on "The Ambassador From the U. S. A.," a story written to order for him by Vincent Sheehan. In between making pictures, Will makes tours around the country, flying his airplane—he is now his own pilot—making

personal appearance at motion picture the-
atres and speaking over the radio. To this
day, he says he never knows what he is going
to say until he steps before the curtain, but
just rambles on and hopes that he will catch
his audiences in the right mood. In Boston,
he once caused tremendous amusement by
informing a gathering that, while they were
proud of having ancestors who came over
on the Mayflower, his ancestors met the
Mayflower when she came in. Again, he
will relate his attempt to add a room to his
home in Beverly Hills, which resulted in
his tearing down the entire house and sell-
ing the land on which it was built.

Will Rogers was married on November
28, 1908, to Betty Blake of Rogers, Arkan-
sas, and is the father of three children: Will,
Mary and James. In 1919 he published
"Rogerisms—The Cowboy Philosopher on

Prohibition," and "Rogerisms—The Cowboy Philosopher on the Peace Conference."
In 1920 came "Rogerisms—What We
Laugh At"; in 1924, "The Illiterate Di-
gest"; and in 1927, "Letters of a Self-Made
Diplomat to His President," and "There's
Not a Bathing Suit in Russia." His income
is said to be one of the largest earned by anyone in this country, yet he does not make any
show about it, and his tastes are simple.
"Who's Who" describes him as author and
actor, but the word, "humorist," is left out.
Sometimes we think that if the United
States had a court, Will Rogers would be
the court jester, but as it is, he amuses
people all over the world, so perhaps it
would be better not to limit him to so narrow a sphere as that of entertaining just an
intimate circle.

INDEX.

329

Index

330

Index

Index

Index

333

Index

334

Index

Index

Index

337

Index

Index

339

Index

341